math
expressions
Common Core

Dr. Karen C. Fuson

 Watch the platypus come alive in its watery world as you discover and solve math challenges.

Download the *Math Worlds AR* app available on Android or iOS devices.

Grade 2

Volume 1

This material is based upon work supported by the
National Science Foundation
under Grant Numbers
ESI-9816320, REC-9806020, and RED-935373.

Any opinions, findings, and conclusions, or recommendations expressed in this material
are those of the author and do not necessarily reflect the views of the National Science Foundation.

Printed in the U.S.A.

ISBN 978-0-544-91974-7

12 13 14 15 16   0607 25 24 23 22

4500851021   D E F G

BIG IDEA 1 - Strategies for Addition and Subtraction

Family Letter 1

Vocabulary Cards 2A

1 Represent Addition and Subtraction 3
2.OA.A.1, 2.OA.B.2, 2.NBT.B.9

Family Letter 7

2 Relate Addition and Subtraction 9
2.OA.A.1, 2.OA.B.2

Math Mountain Cards 9

3 Make-a-Ten Strategies 15
2.OA.B.2, 2.NBT.B.9

Coin Strips 15

4 Relate Unknown Addends and Subtraction 19
2.OA.A.1, 2.OA.B.2, 2.NBT.B.9

5 More Practice with Unknown Addends and Teen Totals 21
2.OA.A.1, 2.OA.B.2, 2.NBT.B.9

6 Odd and Even Numbers 23
2.OA.C.3, 2.NBT.A.2

7 Strategies Using Doubles 27
2.OA.B.2, 2.OA.C.3, 2.NBT.B.9

8 Equations, Equation Chains, and Vertical Form 29
2.OA.B.2

9 Add Three or Four Addends 31
2.OA.A.1, 2.OA.B.2, 2.NBT.B.9

Dive the Deep 31

Quick Quiz 1 35

Fluency Check 1 36

BIG IDEA 2 - Addition and Subtraction Situations

Family Letter 37

10 *Add To* and *Take From* Word Problems 39
2.OA.A.1, 2.OA.B.2, 2.NBT.B.9

11 *Add To* and *Take From* Problems—Unknown in All Positions ... 41
2.OA.A.1, 2.OA.B.2, 2.NBT.B.9

12 *Put Together/Take Apart* Problems 43
2.OA.A.1, 2.OA.B.2

13 Special *Put Together/Take Apart* Problems 45
2.OA.A.1, 2.OA.B.2

14 *Compare* Word Problems 47
2.OA.A.1, 2.OA.B.2

15 More *Compare* Word Problems 49
2.OA.A.1, 2.OA.B.2

16 Mixed Word Problems 51
2.OA.A.1, 2.OA.B.2, 2.NBT.B.9

Green Make-a-Ten Cards 53

Quick Quiz 2 57

Fluency Check 2 58

BIG IDEA 3 - More Complex Situations

17 Problems with Not Enough, Extra, or Hidden Information 59
2.OA.A.1, 2.OA.B.2

18 More Complex *Compare* Problems 63
2.OA.A.1, 2.OA.B.2

19 Two-Step Word Problems 65
2.OA.A.1, 2.OA.B.2

20 Mixed Word Problems 69
2.OA.A.1, 2.OA.B.2, 2.NBT.B.9

Blue Make-a-Ten Cards 71

21 Focus on Mathematical Practices 75
2.OA.A.1, 2.OA.B.2, 2.OA.C.3

Quick Quiz 3 77

Fluency Check 3 78

✓ **UNIT 1 Review/Test** 79

Unit 1 Performance Task 83

© Houghton Mifflin Harcourt Publishing Company

BIG IDEA 1 - Use Place Value

Family Letter 85

Vocabulary Cards 86A

1 Ones, Tens, and Hundreds 87
   2.OA.A.1, 2.NBT.A.1, 2.NBT.A.1.a, 2.NBT.A.2, 2.NBT.A.3

2 Draw Quick Tens and Quick Hundreds 89
   2.OA.A.1, 2.NBT.A.1, 2.NBT.A.1.a, 2.NBT.A.2, 2.NBT.A.3, 2.NBT.B.5, 2.NBT.B.9

   Secret Code Cards (1–100) 89

3 Represent Numbers in Different Ways........................ 93
   2.NBT.A.1, 2.NBT.A.1.a, 2.NBT.A.2, 2.NBT.A.3

4 Combine Ones, Tens, and Hundreds 95
   2.NBT.A.1, 2.NBT.A.1.a, 2.NBT.A.3, 2.NBT.B.5, 2.NBT.B.7, 2.NBT.B.8, 2.NBT.B.9

5 Compare Numbers Within 200.................................... 97
   2.NBT.A.1, 2.NBT.A.3, 2.NBT.A.4

Quick Quiz 1 99

Fluency Check 4 100

BIG IDEA 2 - Add 2-Digit Numbers

Family Letter 101

6 Explore 2-Digit Addition.. 103
   2.OA.A.1, 2.OA.B.2, 2.NBT.A.1, 2.NBT.A.1.a, 2.NBT.B.6, 2.NBT.B.7, 2.NBT.B.9

7 Addition—Show All Totals Method............................. 105
   2.OA.A.1, 2.NBT.A.1, 2.NBT.A.1.a, 2.NBT.B.6, 2.NBT.B.7, 2.NBT.B.9

8 Addition—New Groups Below Method......................... 107
   2.OA.A.1, 2.NBT.A.1, 2.NBT.A.1.a, 2.NBT.B.6, 2.NBT.B.7, 2.NBT.B.9

9 Practice Addition with Sums Over 100 109
   2.NBT.A.1, 2.NBT.A.1.a, 2.NBT.B.6, 2.NBT.B.7, 2.NBT.B.9

10 Choose an Addition Method 111
   2.NBT.A.1, 2.NBT.B.6, 2.NBT.B.7, 2.NBT.B.9

Quick Quiz 2 113

Fluency Check 5 114

BIG IDEA 3 - Money and Fluency for Addition Within 100

11 Buy with Pennies and Dimes 115
2.NBT.A.1, 2.NBT.A.1.a, 2.NBT.B.6, 2.NBT.B.7, 2.MD.C.8

Dollar Bills 115

12 Pennies, Nickels, and Dimes 119
2.NBT.A.2, 2.MD.C.8

13 Fluency: Addition Within 100 123
2.NBT.B.5

New Ten Challenge 125

14 Add Three or Four 2-Digit Addends 127
2.NBT.B.5, 2.NBT.B.6, 2.NBT.B.7

15 Focus on Mathematical Practices 129
2.OA.A.1, 2.NBT.A.2, 2.NBT.A.4, 2.NBT.B.5, 2.NBT.B.6, 2.NBT.B.7, 2.MD.C.8

Quick Quiz 3 131

Fluency Check 6 132

✓ **UNIT 2 Review/Test** 133

Unit 2 Performance Task 137

BIG IDEA 1 - Length and Shapes

Family Letter 139

Vocabulary Cards 140A

1 Measure Length 141
   2.OA.B.2, 2.MD.A.1, 2.MD.A.4

2 Recognize and Draw Shapes.. 145
   2.MD.A.1, 2.MD.A.4, 2.G.A.1

3 Estimate and Measure.. 149
   2.OA.B.2, 2.MD.A.1, 2.MD.A.3, 2.G.A.1

4 Draw, Estimate, and Measure 151
   2.OA.B.2, 2.MD.A.1, 2.MD.A.3, 2.G.A.1

5 Draw Using Faces 153
   2.G.A.1

   Rectangular Prisms 153

Quick Quiz 1 157

Fluency Check 7 158

BIG IDEA 2 - Estimate, Measure, and Make Line Plots

Family Letter 159

6 Estimate and Measure with Centimeters.............................. 161
   2.NBT.B.7, 2.MD.A.1, 2.MD.A.3, 2.MD.A.4, 2.MD.D.9

   Meter Tape (Vertical) 161

7 Estimate and Measure with Inches 167
   2.MD.A.1, 2.MD.A.2, 2.MD.A.3, 2.MD.D.9

   Inch Ruler 167

   Yardstick 171

8 Measure for and Make Line Plots 175
   2.MD.A.1, 2.MD.A.2, 2.MD.A.3, 2.MD.D.9

9 Focus on Mathematical Practices... 179
   2.NBT.B.5, 2.MD.A.1, 2.MD.A.2, 2.G.A.1

Quick Quiz 2 181

Fluency Check 8 182

✓ **UNIT 3 Review/Test** 183

   Unit 3 Performance Task 187

Student Resources

Problem Types S1

Glossary S4

Correlation: Common Core State Standards for
Mathematical Content S19

Correlation: Common Core State Standards for
Mathematical Practice S24

Index S28

Dear Family:

Your child is learning math in a program called *Math Expressions,* which links mathematical ideas to a child's everyday experiences. This helps children understand math better.

In this program, your child will learn math and have fun by

- working with objects and making drawings of math situations.
- listening to and working with other children and sharing ways to solve problems.
- writing and solving problems and connecting math to daily life.
- helping classmates learn.

Your child will have homework almost every day. He or she needs a Homework Helper. The helper may be anyone—a family member, an older brother or sister, a neighbor, or a friend. Set aside a definite time for homework and provide your child with a quiet place to work where there are no distractions. Encourage your child to talk about what is happening in math class. If your child is having problems with math, please talk to me to see how you might help.

Please cut, fill in, and return the bottom part of this letter.

Thank you. You are very important to your child's learning.

Sincerely,
Your child's teacher

✂ -

My child _____ will have
(child's name)

_____ as a Homework Helper.
(name of Homework Helper)

This person is my child's _____.
(relationship to child)

_____
signature of parent or guardian

CC SS Unit 1 addresses the following standards from the Common Core State Standards for Mathematics: **2.OA.A.1, 2.OA.B.2, 2.OA.C.3, 2.NBT.A.2, 2.NBT.B.6, 2.NBT.B.9, and all** Mathematical Practices.

Estimada familia:

Su niño está aprendiendo matemáticas con un programa llamado *Math Expressions,* que relaciona conceptos matemáticos abstractos con la experiencia diaria de los niños. Esto ayuda a los niños a entender mejor las matemáticas.

Con este programa, su niño va a aprender matemáticas y se divertirá mientras:

- trabaja con objetos y hace dibujos de situaciones matemáticas.
- escucha y trabaja con otros estudiantes y comparte con ellos estrategias para resolver problemas.
- escribe y resuelve problemas, y relaciona las matemáticas con la vida diaria.
- ayuda a sus compañeros de clase a aprender.

Su niño tendrá tarea casi todos los días y necesitará que alguna persona lo ayude. Esa persona puede ser, usted, un hermano mayor, un vecino o un amigo. Establezca una hora para la tarea y ofrezca a su niño un lugar donde trabajar sin distracciones. Anímelo a comentar lo que está aprendiendo en la clase de matemáticas. Si él tiene problemas con las matemáticas, hable por favor con el maestro para ver cómo puede usted ayudar.

Por favor recorte, complete y devuelva el formulario al maestro.

Muchas gracias. Usted es imprescindible en el aprendizaje de su niño.

Atentamente,
El maestro de su niño

- -

La persona que ayudará a mi niño _____ es
(nombre del niño)

_____. Esta persona es
(nombre de la persona)

_____ de mi niño.
(relación con el niño)

_____
Su firma

CC SS **En la Unidad 1 se aplican los siguientes estándares de los** Estándares estatales comunes de matemáticas: **2.OA.A.1, 2.OA.B.2, 2.OA.C.3, 2.NBT.A.2, 2.NBT.B.6, 2.NBT.B.9 y todos los de** Prácticas matemáticas.

Represent Addition and Subtraction

addend	doubles minus 2
addition doubles	doubles plus 1
doubles minus 1	doubles plus 2

$7 + 7 = 14$, so
$7 + 5 = 12$, 2 less than 14.

$$5 + 6 = 11$$
↑   ↑
addends

$6 + 6 = 12$, so
$6 + 7 = 13$, 1 more than 12.

Both addends (or partners)
are the same.

$$4 + 4 = 8$$

$6 + 6 = 12$, so
$6 + 8 = 14$, 2 more than 12.

$7 + 7 = 14$, so
$7 + 6 = 13$, 1 less than 14.

equation

extra
information

equation
chain

fewer

even

hidden
information

Franny has 8 kittens and 2 dogs. 4 kittens are asleep. How many kittens are awake?

$$8 - 4 = \boxed{4}$$

The number of dogs is extra information. It is not needed to solve the problem.

$$4 + 3 = 7$$
$$7 = 4 + 3$$
$$9 - 5 = 4$$
$$4 + 5 = 8 + 1$$

An equation must have an = sign.

There are fewer ■ than ▲.

$$3 + 4 = 5 + 2 = 8 - 1 = 7$$

Heather bought a dozen eggs. She used 7 of them to make breakfast. How many eggs does she have left?

$$12 - 7 = \boxed{5}$$

The hidden information is that a dozen means 12.

A number is even if you can make groups of 2 and have none left over.

8 is an even number.

more

pattern

odd

subtraction doubles

pairs

total

This pattern shows counting by 2s.

2, 4, 6, 8, 10

There are more ⬤ than ⬛.

The subtrahend and the difference, or partners, are the same.

$$8 - 4 = 4$$

A number is odd if you can make groups of 2 and have 1 left over.

9 is an odd number.

10 ←—total

8   2

A group of 2 is a pair.

The picture shows 4 pairs of counters.

unknown addend

vertical form

$$3 + \boxed{} = 9$$

$$\uparrow$$

unknown addend

$$\begin{array}{r} 4 \\ +\,3 \\ \hline 7 \end{array}$$

Name _____

Relate Math Mountains and Equations for Addition

VOCABULARY
equation
total
addends

$8 + 6 = \boxed{}$

Discuss the Math Mountain and the **equation**.

1. Where is the **total**? Where are the partners or **addends**?

2. Tell word problems for both.

3. Solve both and compare your strategies.

Relate Math Mountains and Equations for Subtraction

$9 + \boxed{} = 15$

$15 - 9 = \boxed{}$

Discuss this Math Mountain and the equations.

4. Where is the total? Where are the partners or addends?

5. Tell word problems for all.

6. Solve all and compare your strategies.

Count On for Addition or Subtraction

7 For addition, I pretend I already counted 9. Then
I count on 3 more to get the total. I stop when I
see/feel 3. I hear 12, the unknown total.

$9 + 3 = \boxed{12}$

Already ● ● ● Stop when
9   10 11 12 I see/feel 3 more.

$9 + 3 = 12$

11 12
10
Already 9

3 more to
make 12.

8 For subtraction, I pretend I already counted 9.
I count on until I get to 12. I stop when I hear 12.
I see/feel 3, the unknown partner.

$12 - 9 = \boxed{3}$

I took 9   ● ● ●
away.   10 11 12

3 more to
$12 - 9 = 3$ make 12.

I took 9
away.

11 12
10

3 more to
make 12.

Patterns in Equations

9 Discuss patterns in the eight equations for a Math
Mountain with total 12 and partners 9 and 3.

$9 + 3 = 12$ $12 = 9 + 3$

$3 + 9 = 12$ $12 = 3 + 9$

$12 - 9 = 3$ $3 = 12 - 9$

$12 - 3 = 9$ $9 = 12 - 3$

Represent Addition and Subtraction

Write Equations for Math Mountains

Write two equations for each Math Mountain.
Use a ☐ for the unknown number.

10

$$9 + 5 = \boxed{}$$

_____

_____

11

_____

_____

12

_____

_____

13

_____

14

_____

15

_____

Represent Addition and Subtraction **5**

Draw Math Mountains

Draw a Math Mountain and write one more equation.
Use a □ for the unknown number.

 16

$9 + 6 = \boxed{}$

 17

$9 + \boxed{} = 12$

18

$8 + \boxed{} = 16$

 19

$5 + 6 = \boxed{}$

 20

$13 - 4 = \boxed{}$

21

$15 - 7 = \boxed{}$

✔ Check Understanding

Draw one Math Mountain with all three numbers in place.

Represent Addition and Subtraction

Dear Family:

Your child is exploring addition and subtraction equations with Math Mountain Cards. The cards have a large number at the top and two smaller numbers at the bottom. From the cards, children can see that two smaller numbers can be added together to make a larger number. They can also see that a large number can be broken apart into two smaller numbers.

Children will write addition and subtraction equations that they can make from the cards, as shown in the example. The two partners, 9 and 6, can be added to make the total, 15. They can be switched (6 and 9) and still make 15.

$9 + 6 = 15$ $15 = 9 + 6$

$6 + 9 = 15$ $15 = 6 + 9$

$15 - 9 = 6$ $6 = 15 - 9$

$15 - 6 = 9$ $9 = 15 - 6$

15

− −

9 + 6

Children see and write all eight equations. It is important for understanding algebra that they sometimes see equations with only one number on the left.

Please contact me if you need practice materials. Thank you for helping your child learn about the relationship between addition and subtraction.

Sincerely,
Your child's teacher

CC SS Unit 1 addresses the following standards from the Common Core State Standards for Mathematics: **2.OA.A.1, 2.OA.B.2, 2.OA.C.3, 2.NBT.A.2, 2.NBT.B.6, 2.NBT.B.9,** and all Mathematical Practices.

Estimada familia:

Su niño está aprendiendo ecuaciones de suma y resta usando las tarjetas *Math Mountain*. Las tarjetas tienen un número grande en la parte superior y dos números más pequeños en la parte inferior. En las tarjetas los niños pueden ver que se pueden sumar dos números más pequeños para obtener un número más grande. También pueden ver que un número grande se puede separar en dos números más pequeños.

Los niños escribirán ecuaciones de suma y resta que puedan hacer a partir de las tarjetas, según se muestra en el ejemplo. Se pueden sumar las dos partes, 9 y 6, para obtener el total, 15. También se pueden intercambiar (6 y 9) y todavía obtener 15.

$9 + 6 = 15$

$6 + 9 = 15$

$15 - 9 = 6$

$15 - 6 = 9$

15

— —

9 + 6

$15 = 9 + 6$

$15 = 6 + 9$

$6 = 15 - 9$

$9 = 15 - 6$

Los niños ven y escriben las ocho ecuaciones. Para comprender álgebra es importante que vean ecuaciones con un solo número a la izquierda.

Por favor comuníquese conmigo si necesita materiales para practicar. Gracias por ayudar a su niño a aprender la relación entre suma y resta.

Atentamente,
El maestro de su niño

CC SS **En la Unidad 1 se aplican los siguientes estándares de los** Estándares estatales comunes de matemáticas: **2.OA.A.1, 2.OA.B.2, 2.OA.C.3, 2.NBT.A.2, 2.NBT.B.6, 2.NBT.B.9 y todos los de** Prácticas matemáticas.

© Houghton Mifflin Harcourt Publishing Company

Math Mountain Cards

Math Mountain Cards

Math Mountain Cards

Name _____

Add and Subtract with Math Mountains

Complete the Math Mountain to solve
the problem. Complete the equation.

---

1 Vicki has 8 stickers.
She gives 2 stickers to Judy.
How many stickers does
Vicki have now?

$8 - 2 = \boxed{}$ stickers

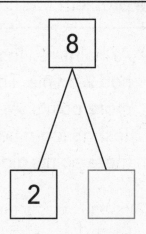

---

2 At the park, Rashad counts
4 birds. His sister counts
5 birds. How many birds do
they count together?

$4 + 5 = \boxed{}$ birds

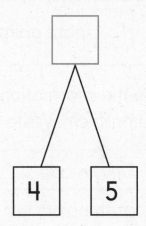

---

3 Odalis played on the computer
for 10 minutes. Liam played on
the computer for 3 fewer minutes
than Odalis. How many minutes
did Liam play on the computer?

$\boxed{} - \boxed{} = \boxed{}$ minutes

Add and Subtract with Math Mountains (continued)

Complete the Math Mountain to solve the problem. Complete the equation.

---

4 At halftime, Tasha's soccer team had 2 points. Then they scored some more points. At the end of the game, Tasha's team had 5 points. How many more points did Tasha's team score?

□ + □ = □

□ more points

Use the information in the Math Mountain to complete the problem. Write the equation.

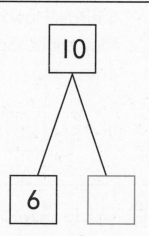

5 Devy made _____ bookmarks to sell at the craft fair last weekend. He sold _____ bookmarks on Saturday. How many bookmarks did Devy have left to sell on Sunday?

□ − □ = □ bookmarks

✓ **Check Understanding**
Draw a Math Mountain. Write one addition equation and one subtraction equation for that Math Mountain.

Relate Addition and Subtraction

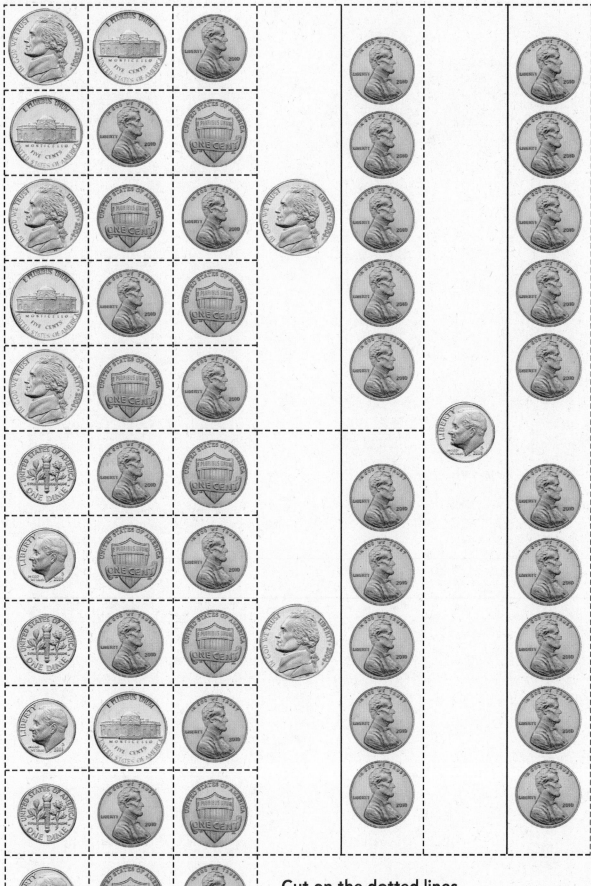

Cut on the dotted lines.
Fold on the solid lines.

Coin Strips

Name _____

Make a Ten to Solve

Make a ten to solve. Draw to show your work.
Complete the make-a-ten equation.

---

1 $7 + 4 =$ ☐ $\boxed{10} + $ ☐ $= $ ☐

---

2 $5 + 8 =$ ☐   ☐ $+$ ☐ $=$ ☐

---

3 $3 + 9 =$ ☐   ☐ $+$ ☐ $=$ ☐

---

4 $7 + 6 =$ ☐   ☐ $+$ ☐ $=$ ☐

---

5 $6 + 8 =$ ☐   ☐ $+$ ☐ $=$ ☐

---

6 $9 + 7 =$ ☐   ☐ $+$ ☐ $=$ ☐

CC SS Content Standards **2.OA.B.2, 2.NBT.B.9**
Mathematical Practices **MP1, MP7**

Make a Ten with Math Mountains

Complete the Math Mountain.
Write the make-a-ten Math Mountain.

7

8

9

✔ **Check Understanding**

Show and explain how to use the Make-a-Ten strategy to solve $7 + 5$.

Make-a-Ten Strategies

VOCABULARY
unknown addend

Find the Unknown Addend

$7 + \boxed{5} = 12$

10

$7 \bullet\bullet\bullet | \bullet\bullet$

$3 + 2 = 5$

$12 - 7 = \boxed{5}$

$\bullet\bullet\bullet\bullet\bullet\bullet\bullet \; \bullet\bullet \; | \; \bullet\bullet\bullet \; \bullet\bullet$

7   5

Find the **unknown addend** (unknown partner).

1 $8 + \boxed{} = 11$ $15 - 6 = \boxed{}$ $8 + \boxed{} = 14$

---

2 $7 + \boxed{} = 13$ $12 - 8 = \boxed{}$ $3 + \boxed{} = 12$

---

3 $5 + \boxed{} = 14$ $16 - 9 = \boxed{}$ $9 + \boxed{} = 17$

---

4 $9 + \boxed{} = 14$ $18 - 9 = \boxed{}$ $7 + \boxed{} = 11$

---

5 $8 + \boxed{} = 13$ $13 - 9 = \boxed{}$ $15 - \boxed{} = 8$

13   13   15

8 $\boxed{}$ 9 $\boxed{}$ $\boxed{}$ 8

---

6 Find the partner for $11 - 6 = \boxed{}$.

Make a math drawing to show what you did.

CC SS Content Standards **2.OA.B.2, 2.NBT.B.9**
Mathematical Practices **MP1**

Practice Finding Teen Totals and Unknown Addends

Are we looking for a partner or total?
Circle the P or the T for each column.

Then write each partner or total.

	P or T	P or T	P or T
7	$5 + 8 = \boxed{}$	$7 + \boxed{} = 11$	$11 - 9 = \boxed{}$
8	$4 + 8 = \boxed{}$	$9 + \boxed{} = 17$	$16 - 8 = \boxed{}$
9	$7 + 9 = \boxed{}$	$7 + \boxed{} = 12$	$13 - 7 = \boxed{}$
10	$5 + 6 = \boxed{}$	$8 + \boxed{} = 16$	$14 - 7 = \boxed{}$
11	$8 + 3 = \boxed{}$	$9 + \boxed{} = 18$	$14 - 9 = \boxed{}$
12	$8 + 4 = \boxed{}$	$6 + \boxed{} = 15$	$12 - 5 = \boxed{}$

© Houghton Mifflin Harcourt Publishing Company

✓ **Check Understanding**

Explain how to use the Make-a-Ten strategy to find the unknown addend below.

$8 + \boxed{} = 13$

Relate Unknown Addends and Subtraction

Name _____

Equation Pairs and Math Mountains

Find the unknown addend. Draw to show your work.
Complete the Math Mountain.

1   8 + ☐ = 15

15 − 8 = ☐

---

2   6 + ☐ = 15

15 − 6 = ☐

---

3   7 + ☐ = 12

12 − 7 = ☐

Unknown Addends and Equation Pairs

Read the problem. Write an unknown addend
equation and a subtraction equation to solve.

4 Tally ate 8 cherries. Rita ate some
cherries. Together, they ate 12 cherries.
How many cherries did Rita eat?

$8 + \boxed{} = 12$

$12 - \boxed{} = 8$

_____ cherries

---

5 Rey gathered some daisies. Ben
gave Rey 6 more daisies. Now
Rey has 13 daisies. How many
daisies did Rey gather?

$\boxed{} + 6 = 13$

$13 - \boxed{} = 6$

_____ daisies

---

6 Aziz told some jokes. His cousin Harris
told the same number of jokes. In all,
they told 18 jokes. How many jokes did
each boy tell?

$9 + \boxed{} = 18$

$18 - \boxed{} = 9$

_____ jokes

✓ **Check Understanding**

Explain how unknown addend equations
and subtraction equations are the same.

More Practice with Unknown Addends and Teen Totals

Name _____

VOCABULARY
pairs

Count by 2s

1 Loop **pairs** of jars.

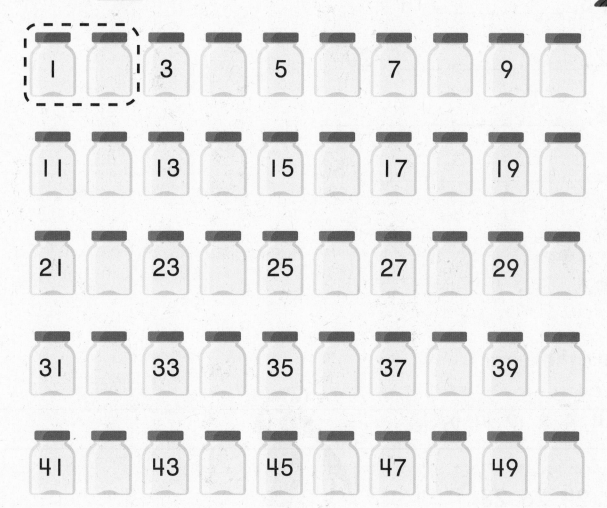

1		3		5		7		9	
11		13		15		17		19	
21		23		25		27		29	
31		33		35		37		39	
41		43		45		47		49	

2 Number the jars from 1 to 50.

3 Count by 2s from 2 to 50.

2, ____, 6, ____, 10, ____, ____, 16, ____, ____,

____, 24, ____, ____, ____, ____, ____, 36, ____,

____, ____, ____, ____, ____, 50

Patterns

VOCABULARY
pattern

Count by 2s to complete each **pattern**.

④ 6, 8, _____, _____, 14

⑤ 12, _____, _____, _____, 20

⑥ 26, _____, _____, _____, _____

⑦ _____, _____, _____, _____, 50

⑧ 50, _____, _____, _____, 58

⑨ 76, _____, _____, _____, _____

What's the Error?

2, 4, 6, 8, 12, 14, 16, 18,

22, 24, 26, 28

I counted by 2s to 28. Did I count correctly?

⑩ Show how to count by 2s from 2 to 28.

2, _____, _____, _____, _____,

_____, _____, _____, _____, _____,

_____, _____, _____, 28

Odd and Even Numbers

Name _____

Make Pairs

Draw lines to make pairs.
Circle **odd** or **even**.

VOCABULARY
odd
even

11

odd   even

12

odd   even

13

odd   even

14

odd   even

15

odd   even

16

odd   even

17

odd   even

18

odd   even

19

odd   even

20

odd   even

Make Equal Groups

Try to make equal groups.
Circle odd or even.

VOCABULARY
addition doubles

21 9

odd   even

22 6

odd   even

23 12

odd   even

24 7

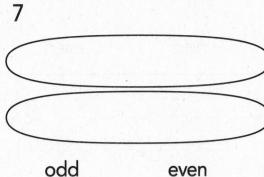

odd   even

Write Addition Doubles

Complete the **addition doubles** equation.

25 $\boxed{} + \boxed{} = 8$

26 $\boxed{} + \boxed{} = 10$

27 $\boxed{} + \boxed{} = 18$

28 $\boxed{} + \boxed{} = 16$

 Check Understanding

Show or write two ways to decide if 6 is *even* or *odd*.

Odd and Even Numbers

Name _____

Use Doubles

Addition Doubles and **Subtraction Doubles**	**Doubles Plus 1** and **Doubles Minus 1**	**Doubles Plus 2** and **Doubles Minus 2**
1 $5 + 5 = \boxed{}$ $10 - 5 = \boxed{}$	$5 + 6 = \boxed{}$ $5 + 4 = \boxed{}$	$5 + 7 = \boxed{}$ $5 + 3 = \boxed{}$
2 $6 + 6 = \boxed{}$ $12 - 6 = \boxed{}$	$6 + 7 = \boxed{}$ $6 + 5 = \boxed{}$	$6 + 8 = \boxed{}$ $6 + 4 = \boxed{}$
3 $7 + 7 = \boxed{}$ $14 - 7 = \boxed{}$	$7 + 8 = \boxed{}$ $7 + 6 = \boxed{}$	$7 + 9 = \boxed{}$ $7 + 5 = \boxed{}$
4 $8 + 8 = \boxed{}$ $16 - 8 = \boxed{}$	$8 + 9 = \boxed{}$ $8 + 7 = \boxed{}$	$8 + 10 = \boxed{}$ $8 + 6 = \boxed{}$
5 $9 + 9 = \boxed{}$ $18 - 9 = \boxed{}$	$9 + 10 = \boxed{}$ $9 + 8 = \boxed{}$	$9 + 11 = \boxed{}$ $9 + 7 = \boxed{}$

Use Doubles (continued)

Add. Use doubles.

6 $9 + 9 =$ ☐ $8 + 6 =$ ☐ $6 + 5 =$ ☐

7 $7 + 7 =$ ☐ $7 + 6 =$ ☐ $9 + 11 =$ ☐

8 $11 + 9 =$ ☐ $6 + 8 =$ ☐ $6 + 6 =$ ☐

9 $7 + 9 =$ ☐ $5 + 5 =$ ☐ $8 + 7 =$ ☐

10 $9 + 8 =$ ☐ $5 + 7 =$ ☐ $6 + 4 =$ ☐

11 $8 + 8 =$ ☐ $8 + 10 =$ ☐ $9 + 7 =$ ☐

12 $5 + 4 =$ ☐ $6 + 7 =$ ☐ $5 + 6 =$ ☐

13 $7 + 8 =$ ☐ $8 + 9 =$ ☐ $7 + 5 =$ ☐

✔ Check Understanding
Describe two ways of using doubles to add $8 + 6$.

Strategies Using Doubles

Name _____

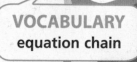

VOCABULARY
equation chain

What's the Error?

① Help Puzzled Penguin.

$6 + 3 = \boxed{9} - 5$

Did I make a mistake?

Use Equations to Make an Equation Chain

② Solve the equations.
If the answer is 8, color the block 🖍 .

$8 + 9 = \square$	$12 - 6 = \square$	$7 + 5 = \square$
$5 + 3 = \square$	$17 - 9 = \square$	$13 - 5 = \square$
$5 + 4 = \square$	$1 + 7 = \square$	$15 - 8 = \square$
$11 - 3 = \square$	$4 + 4 = \square$	$3 + 8 = \square$
$16 - 8 = \square$	$6 + 6 = \square$	$5 + 7 = \square$

③ Use the blocks you colored to make an **equation chain**.

_____

_____

VOCABULARY
vertical form

Show Three Ways

Write the equation, the **vertical form**, and the Math Mountain.
Use a ☐ to show the unknown number.

④ 8 and 5 make how many?

_____

⑤ 7 and what number make 15?

_____

⑥ 18 take away 8 equals what number?

_____

⑦ 17 minus 8 makes what number?

✓ **Check Understanding**

Write 7 + 5 = ☐ in vertical form. Then find the total.

Equations, Equation Chains, and Vertical Form

Dive the Deep

$11 - 6 = \boxed{5}$ $12 - \boxed{6} = 6$ $13 - 8 = \boxed{5}$

$12 - 7 = \boxed{5}$ $17 - \boxed{8} = 9$ $15 - 6 = \boxed{9}$

$12 - 9 = \boxed{3}$ $13 - \boxed{5} = 8$ $11 - 9 = \boxed{2}$

$13 - 4 = \boxed{9}$ $14 - \boxed{6} = 8$ $13 - 9 = \boxed{4}$

$11 - 5 = \boxed{6}$ $17 - \boxed{9} = 8$ $15 - 7 = \boxed{8}$

$14 - 9 = \boxed{5}$ $11 - \boxed{8} = 3$ $14 - 8 = \boxed{6}$

$14 - 7 = \boxed{7}$ $12 - \boxed{4} = 8$ $12 - 5 = \boxed{7}$

$16 - 7 = \boxed{9}$ $16 - \boxed{8} = 8$ $11 - 3 = \boxed{8}$

$11 - 7 = \boxed{4}$ $15 - \boxed{7} = 8$ $13 - 6 = \boxed{7}$

$12 - 3 = \boxed{9}$ $16 - \boxed{9} = 7$ $18 - 9 = \boxed{9}$

$13 - 7 = \boxed{6}$ $11 - \boxed{4} = 7$ $12 - 8 = \boxed{4}$

Dive the Deep

$11 - 5 = \boxed{6}$ | $12 - \boxed{6} = 6$ | $13 - 5 = \boxed{8}$

$12 - 5 = \boxed{7}$ | $17 - \boxed{9} = 8$ | $15 - 9 = \boxed{6}$

$12 - 3 = \boxed{9}$ | $13 - \boxed{8} = 5$ | $11 - 2 = \boxed{9}$

$13 - 9 = \boxed{4}$ | $14 - \boxed{8} = 6$ | $13 - 4 = \boxed{9}$

$11 - 6 = \boxed{5}$ | $17 - \boxed{8} = 9$ | $15 - 8 = \boxed{7}$

$14 - 5 = \boxed{9}$ | $11 - \boxed{3} = 8$ | $14 - 6 = \boxed{8}$

$14 - 7 = \boxed{7}$ | $12 - \boxed{8} = 4$ | $12 - 7 = \boxed{5}$

$16 - 9 = \boxed{7}$ | $16 - \boxed{8} = 8$ | $11 - 8 = \boxed{3}$

$11 - 4 = \boxed{7}$ | $15 - \boxed{8} = 7$ | $13 - 7 = \boxed{6}$

$12 - 9 = \boxed{3}$ | $16 - \boxed{7} = 9$ | $18 - 9 = \boxed{9}$

$13 - 6 = \boxed{7}$ | $11 - \boxed{7} = 4$ | $12 - 4 = \boxed{8}$

Dive the Deep

Name _____

Find a Sum of 10

Circle the two addends that make ten. Then write the total.

1 $6 + 9 + 1 = \boxed{}$

2 $5 + 7 + 3 = \boxed{}$

3 $5 + 9 + 5 = \boxed{}$

4 $6 + 4 + 7 = \boxed{}$

5 $4 + 1 + 6 = \boxed{}$

6 $1 + 9 + 4 = \boxed{}$

7 $3 + 2 + 8 = \boxed{}$

8 $3 + 2 + 7 = \boxed{}$

Add in Any Order

Write the total.

9 $9 + 3 + 5 = \boxed{}$

10 $9 + 7 + 2 = \boxed{}$

11 $8 + 9 + 2 = \boxed{}$

12 $7 + 8 + 5 = \boxed{}$

13 $7 + 5 + 2 = \boxed{}$

14 $7 + 7 + 2 = \boxed{}$

15 $3 + 9 + 6 = \boxed{}$

16 $3 + 8 + 2 = \boxed{}$

Add Four Addends

Add in any order. Write the sum.

17 $4 + 4 + 5 + 2 =$ ☐

18 $8 + 8 + 5 + 2 =$ ☐

19 $5 + 5 + 3 + 9 =$ ☐

20 $3 + 6 + 5 + 4 =$ ☐

21 $4 + 8 + 9 + 3 =$ ☐

22 $1 + 8 + 8 + 4 =$ ☐

PATH to FLUENCY Add and Subtract Within 20

Add.

23 $6 + 8 =$ _____

24 $9 + 9 =$ _____

25 $7 + 0 =$ _____

26 $\begin{array}{r} 9 \\ + 7 \\ \hline \end{array}$

27 $\begin{array}{r} 8 \\ + 5 \\ \hline \end{array}$

28 $\begin{array}{r} 8 \\ + 2 \\ \hline \end{array}$

29 $\begin{array}{r} 9 \\ + 9 \\ \hline \end{array}$

Subtract.

30 $\begin{array}{r} 15 \\ - 8 \\ \hline \end{array}$

31 $\begin{array}{r} 9 \\ - 7 \\ \hline \end{array}$

32 $\begin{array}{r} 9 \\ - 0 \\ \hline \end{array}$

33 $\begin{array}{r} 12 \\ - 4 \\ \hline \end{array}$

 Check Understanding

Which two numbers did you add first in Exercise 20?

_____

Which two numbers did you add first in Exercise 22?

_____

Add Three or Four Addends

Add or subtract.

1   1 4
      − 9
    _____

_____

2 ☐ = 8 + 6

_____

3 9 + 5 + 1 + 4 = ☐

_____

Find the unknown addend.

4 8 + ☐ = 17

_____

5 Is the number of dots odd or even?

odd   even

Name _____ **Date** _____

Add or subtract.

1 $6 - 2 = \boxed{}$ **2** $11 - 6 = \boxed{}$ **3** $7 - 4 = \boxed{}$

4 $4 + 0 = \boxed{}$ **5** $5 + 1 = \boxed{}$ **6** $6 + 2 = \boxed{}$

7
$$\begin{array}{r} 15 \\ -7 \\ \hline \end{array}$$

8
$$\begin{array}{r} 17 \\ -0 \\ \hline \end{array}$$

9
$$\begin{array}{r} 14 \\ -6 \\ \hline \end{array}$$

10
$$\begin{array}{r} 10 \\ +6 \\ \hline \end{array}$$

11
$$\begin{array}{r} 8 \\ +1 \\ \hline \end{array}$$

12
$$\begin{array}{r} 13 \\ +7 \\ \hline \end{array}$$

13
$$\begin{array}{r} 18 \\ -9 \\ \hline \end{array}$$

14
$$\begin{array}{r} 15 \\ -10 \\ \hline \end{array}$$

15
$$\begin{array}{r} 19 \\ -17 \\ \hline \end{array}$$

Dear Family:

Your child is learning to solve word problems called *Add To* and *Take From* problems. These problems begin with a quantity that is then modified by change—something is added or subtracted—which results in a new quantity.

Proof drawings show what your child was thinking when solving the problem. It is important that children label their drawings to link them to the problem situation.

Add To Problem

Joe has 9 toy cars.
Then he gets 3 more.
How many toy cars does he have now?

$9 + 3 = \boxed{12}$
has gets now

$\boxed{12}$ now

has 9   3 gets

9

$9 + 3 = \boxed{12}$

Take From Problem

Sue has 12 books.
Then she gives her friend 9 books.
How many books does Sue have now?

$12 - 9 = \boxed{3}$
has gives now

has 12

gives 9 $\boxed{3}$ now

has 12
gives 9

10 11 12

$\boxed{3}$ now

Please contact me if you have any questions or concerns.

Sincerely,
Your child's teacher

© Houghton Mifflin Harcourt Publishing Company

CC SS Unit 1 addresses the following standards from the Common Core State Standards for Mathematics: **2.OA.A.1, 2.OA.B.2, 2.OA.C.3, 2.NBT.A.2, 2.NBT.B.6, 2.NBT.B.9,** and all Mathematical Practices.

Estimada familia:

Su niño está aprendiendo a resolver problemas conocidos como problemas de *cambio al sumar* o de *cambio al restar*. Estos empiezan con una cantidad que luego es modificada por un cambio (algo que se suma o se resta), lo que resulta en una nueva cantidad.

Los dibujos muestran lo que su niño estaba pensando mientras resolvía el problema. Es importante que los niños rotulen sus dibujos para relacionarlos con la situación del problema.

Problema de *Cambio al sumar*

José tenía 9 carros de juguete.
Luego recibió 3 más.
¿Cuántos carros de juguete tiene ahora?

9 + 3 = ⌑12⌑
tenía   recibió   ahora

12 ahora
tenía 9   3 recibió

9
9 + 3 = ⌑12⌑

Problema de *Cambio al restar*

Susana tenía 12 libros.
Luego le dio 9 libros a su amigo.
¿Cuántos libros tiene ahora Susana?

12 − 9 = ⌑3⌑
tenía   dio   ahora

tenía 12
dio 9   ⌑3⌑ ahora

tenía 12   o o o
dio 9   10 11 12
      ⌑3⌑ ahora

Si tiene alguna pregunta o algún comentario, por favor comuníquese conmigo.

Atentamente,
El maestro de su niño

En la Unidad 1 se aplican los siguientes estándares de los Estándares estatales comunes de matemáticas: **2.OA.A.1, 2.OA.B.2, 2.OA.C.3, 2.NBT.A.2, 2.NBT.B.6, 2.NBT.B.9 y todos los de** Prácticas matemáticas.

Name _____

Solve and Discuss

Make a drawing. Write an equation.
Solve the problem.

1 The school has 5 computers in the library. They buy some more computers. Now there are 12. How many computers does the school buy?

school

☐ _____
      label

2 Alina has 17 beads. She uses 9 of them to make a bracelet. How many beads does she have left?

beads

☐ _____
      label

3 Erin buys 6 party favors. She needs to buy 15 favors in all. How many favors does she still need to buy?

party favors

☐ _____
      label

Solve and Discuss (continued)

Make a drawing. Write an equation.
Solve the problem.

4 There are 16 children at the playground.
Some children go home. Now there
are 7 children at the playground.
How many children went home?

children

☐ _____
    label

5 Lila has 6 stickers. Sam gives her
some more stickers. Now Lila has
14 stickers. How many stickers does
Sam give Lila?

sticker

☐ _____
    label

6 There are 5 deer in the forest. 6 more
deer enter the forest. How many deer
are in the forest now?

forest

☐ _____
    label

 Check Understanding

Choose one of the problems from this page. Write
the equation a different way.

Add To and Take From Word Problems

Solve and Discuss

Make a drawing. Write an equation.
Solve the problem.

1. Moshe has 5 toy cars. Mary gives him
7 more toy cars. How many toy cars
does Moshe have now?

car

☐ _____
   label

2. Heather buys 5 puzzles at a yard sale.
Then her brother gives her some more.
Now she has a total of 11 puzzles.
How many puzzles did Heather's
brother give her?

puzzle

☐ _____
   label

3. The cook has 16 bags of potatoes.
He uses some to make potato salad.
Now he has 7 bags of potatoes left.
How many bags did he use?

potatoes

☐ _____
   label

Solve and Discuss (continued)

Make a drawing. Write an equation.
Solve the problem.

---

4 Charisa buys 4 new books. Now she has 13 books. How many books did Charisa have before?

book

▢ _____
       label

---

5 Shahla has 16 dolls. She gives 8 dolls to her sister. How many dolls does Shahla have now?

doll

▢ _____
       label

---

6 Brian has some tomato plants in his garden. 9 of the plants are eaten by worms. 4 plants are left. How many plants did Brian have in the beginning?

worm

▢ _____
       label

 Check Understanding

Explain how you represented the problem situation in Problem 4.

     Add To and *Take From* Problems—Unknown in All Positions

Solve and Discuss

Make a drawing. Write an equation.
Solve the problem.

---

1 There are 13 people in a bike race. 8 people are on top of the hill. The rest are at the bottom of the hill. How many people are at the bottom of the hill?

hill

☐ _____
    label

---

2 4 horses are in the barn. 8 horses are in the field. How many horses are on the farm altogether?

horse

☐ _____
    label

---

3 Andrew makes some sandwiches. 6 are turkey sandwiches and 7 are ham sandwiches. How many sandwiches does Andrew make in all?

sandwich

☐ _____
    label

---

4 Keisha has 11 cousins. 4 are boys and the rest are girls. How many are girls?

girl

☐ _____
    label

Solve and Discuss (continued)

Make a drawing. Write an equation.
Solve the problem.

---

5 There are 7 books on the shelf and
5 books on the table. How many books
are there?

book

☐ _____
          label

---

6 Mandy sews 8 blue beads and 6 red
beads on a ribbon. How many beads
are on the ribbon?

ribbon

☐ _____
          label

---

7 Lisa has 5 green pencils and some
yellow pencils. She has 13 pencils in all.
How many yellow pencils does Lisa have?

pencil

☐ _____
          label

✓ **Check Understanding**

Circle the correct answer for each exercise.

In problem 5, the unknown is the   total. / part.

In problem 6, the unknown is the   total. / part.

In problem 7, the unknown is the   total. / part.

Put Together/Take Apart Problems

Name _____

Solve and Discuss

Make a drawing. Write an equation.
Solve the problem.

1. Teodor has 12 flowers in a vase. 8 are daisies.
The rest are roses. How many flowers are roses?

☐
_____
label

rose

2. There are 13 animals at the animal shelter.
7 of them are dogs. The rest are cats.
How many cats are at the shelter?

☐
_____
label

animal
shelter

3. Walt saw 4 crows. Then he saw some
finches at the feeder. He saw 12 birds in all.
How many finches did Walt see?

☐
_____
label

finch

You Decide

Complete this problem.

4. Juana has 4 _____ and Bill

has 6 _____. How many

_____ do they have altogether?

☐
_____
label

© Houghton Mifflin Harcourt Publishing Company

Both Addends Unknown

5 Saira wants to put 7 flowers in a vase. She wants to use lilies and tulips. How many of each flower could she use?

☐ and ☐ $7 = ☐ + ☐$
lilies tulips

☐ and ☐ $7 = ☐ + ☐$
lilies tulips

☐ and ☐ $7 = ☐ + ☐$
lilies tulips

☐ and ☐ $7 = ☐ + ☐$
lilies tulips

☐ and ☐ $7 = ☐ + ☐$
lilies tulips

☐ and ☐ $7 = ☐ + ☐$
lilies tulips

✓ **Check Understanding**
Group some classroom items. Name the group.

VOCABULARY
more
fewer

Solve and Discuss

Make a matching drawing or draw comparison bars.
Write an equation. Solve the problem.

1 Ben has 11 library books. If Ben
returns 4 books, he will have as many
library books as Dale. How many
library books does Dale have?

library

☐ _____
      label

2 Shelley washes 14 toy cars. Amir washes
9 toy cars. How many **more** toy cars
does Shelley wash than Amir?

toy car

☐ _____
      label

3 Gale has 6 peaches in a basket. If Gale gets
5 more peaches, he will have as many peaches
as Carl. How many peaches does Carl have?

basket

☐ _____
      label

4 Rob has 12 markers. Ann has 5 **fewer** markers
than Rob. How many markers does Ann have?

marker

☐ _____
      label

Solve and Discuss (continued)

Make a matching drawing or draw comparison bars.
Write an equation. Solve the problem.

5 Helena has 8 toys. If she gets 3 more, she will
have as many toys as Matt. How many toys
does Matt have?

toy

☐ _____
label

6 Martin has 14 plants in his garden.
Jacob has 5 fewer plants than Martin.
How many plants does Jacob have?

garden

☐ _____
label

PATH to FLUENCY Add and Subtract Within 20

Add.

7 5 + 6 = ☐   8 8 + 7 = ☐   9 13 + 0 = ☐

Subtract.

10 14 − 6 = ☐   11 12 − 3 = ☐   12 11 − 9 = ☐

✓ **Check Understanding**
Explain how comparison bars can be used
to represent one of the word problems on
this page.

Compare Word Problems

Name _____

Solve and Discuss

Make a drawing. Write an equation.
Solve the problem.

---

1 Bo has 13 books in her bag. Gabrielle
has 8 books in her bag. How many fewer
books does Gabrielle have in her bag
than Bo?

book

☐ _____
　　　　label

---

2 Alani has 11 stickers. Nat has 3 stickers.
How many fewer stickers does Nat have
than Alani?

sticker

☐ _____
　　　　label

---

3 An eraser costs 7 cents. A pencil costs
9 cents more than an eraser. How many
cents does a pencil cost?

pencil

☐ _____
　　　　label

---

4 Linda has 11 cherries. If she eats 4 cherries,
she will have the same number as Collis.
How many cherries does Collis have?

cherries

☐ _____
　　　　label

CC SS Content Standards **2.OA.A.1, 2.OA.B.2**
Mathematical Practices **MP3, MP6**

Solve and Discuss (continued)

Make a drawing. Write an equation.
Solve the problem.

5 Idris has 8 notebooks. He has to get 6 more
notebooks to have as many as Ben.
How many notebooks does Ben have?

notebook

☐ _____
      label

6 Rasha solves 3 more puzzles than Leena.
Leena solves 9 puzzles. How many
puzzles does Rasha solve?

puzzle

☐ _____
      label

What's the Error?

Latoya has 12 buttons. If she gives away 5 buttons,
she will have as many as Ron. How many buttons
does Ron have?

Did I make
a mistake?

7 Draw comparison bars to help
Puzzled Penguin.

✔ **Check Understanding**

Choose one problem from this lesson.
Draw comparison bars to show the information
in that problem.

More *Compare* Word Problems

Name _____

Solve and Discuss

Make a drawing. Write an equation.
Solve the problem.

___

1 Erica has 13 color pencils. She
has 8 at home and some at school.
How many are at school?

school

☐ _____
          label

___

2 Joan has 15 toy dinosaurs. Delia has
7 toy dinosaurs. How many fewer toy
dinosaurs does Delia have than Joan?

dinosaur

☐ _____
          label

___

3 Ed has 14 puppets. He gives
some to his brother. Now Ed has
5 puppets left. How many puppets
does Ed give to his brother?

puppet

☐ _____
          label

___

4 Yolanda has a box of tennis balls.
Alvin takes 7 of them. Now Yolanda
has 5 left. How many tennis balls does
Yolanda have in the beginning?

tennis ball

☐ _____
          label

___

© Houghton Mifflin Harcourt Publishing Company

Solve and Discuss (continued)

Make a drawing. Write an equation.
Solve the problem.

---

5 Meena has 6 cherries. Anika
gives her some more cherries. Meena
has 13 cherries now. How many cherries
does Anika give Meena?

cherries

☐ _____
　　　　　label

---

6 Lisha wants to put 15 apples in a bowl.
She wants to use green apples and red
apples. How many of each could she use?
Show three answers.

bowl

☐ green apples and ☐ red apples

☐ green apples and ☐ red apples

☐ green apples and ☐ red apples

✓ **Check Understanding**

Complete these statements about Problem 5.

_____ is the whole.

_____ is a part.

_____ is a part.

Mixed Word Problems

$5 + 7 = \square$

$6 + 7 = \square$

$9 + 9 = \square$

$8 + 7 = \square$

$9 + 7 = \square$

$3 + 8 = \square$

$4 + 8 = \square$

$5 + 8 = \square$

$6 + 8 = \square$

$7 + 8 = \square$

$8 + 8 = \square$

$9 + 8 = \square$

$3 + 9 = \square$

$4 + 9 = \square$

$5 + 9 = \square$

9 + 9 = $\boxed{18}$

9	•	•••••

9 + 1 + 8

6 + 7 = $\boxed{13}$

7	•••	•••

7 + 3 + 3

5 + 7 = $\boxed{12}$

7	•••	••

7 + 3 + 2

3 + 8 = $\boxed{11}$

8	••	•

8 + 2 + 1

9 + 7 = $\boxed{16}$

9	•	•••••

9 + 1 + 6

8 + 7 = $\boxed{15}$

8	••	•••••

8 + 2 + 5

6 + 8 = $\boxed{14}$

8	••	••••

8 + 2 + 4

5 + 8 = $\boxed{13}$

8	••	•••

8 + 2 + 3

4 + 8 = $\boxed{12}$

8	••	••

8 + 2 + 2

9 + 8 = $\boxed{17}$

9	•	••••••

9 + 1 + 7

8 + 8 = $\boxed{16}$

8	••	••••••

8 + 2 + 6

7 + 8 = $\boxed{15}$

8	••	•••••

8 + 2 + 5

5 + 9 = $\boxed{14}$

9	•	••••

9 + 1 + 4

4 + 9 = $\boxed{13}$

9	•	•••

9 + 1 + 3

3 + 9 = $\boxed{12}$

9	•	••

9 + 1 + 2

Green Make-a-Ten Cards

6+9=☐   7+9=☐   7+4=☐

8+4=☐   9+4=☐   6+5=☐

7+5=☐   8+5=☐   9+5=☐

5+6=☐   8+9=☐   7+6=☐

8+6=☐   9+6=☐   4+7=☐

$7 + 4 = \boxed{11}$

| 7 | ••• | • |

7 + 3 + 1

$7 + 9 = \boxed{16}$

| 9 | • | ••••• |

9 + 1 + 6

$6 + 9 = \boxed{15}$

| 9 | • | ••••• |

9 + 1 + 5

$6 + 5 = \boxed{11}$

| 6 | •••• | • |

6 + 4 + 1

$9 + 4 = \boxed{13}$

| 9 | • | ••• |

9 + 1 + 3

$8 + 4 = \boxed{12}$

| 8 | •• | •• |

8 + 2 + 2

$9 + 5 = \boxed{14}$

| 9 | • | •••• |

9 + 1 + 4

$8 + 5 = \boxed{13}$

| 8 | •• | ••• |

8 + 2 + 3

$7 + 5 = \boxed{12}$

| 7 | ••• | •• |

7 + 3 + 2

$7 + 6 = \boxed{13}$

| 7 | ••• | ••• |

7 + 3 + 3

$8 + 9 = \boxed{17}$

| 9 | • | •••••• |

9 + 1 + 7

$5 + 6 = \boxed{11}$

| 6 | •••• | • |

6 + 4 + 1

$4 + 7 = \boxed{11}$

| 7 | ••• | • |

7 + 3 + 1

$9 + 6 = \boxed{15}$

| 9 | • | ••••• |

9 + 1 + 5

$8 + 6 = \boxed{14}$

| 8 | •• | •••• |

8 + 2 + 4

Green Make-a-Ten Cards

Solve.

1 Jon has some baseball cards. He buys 6 more. Now he has 14 baseball cards. How many baseball cards did Jon have at first?

☐ _____
label

2 There are 13 children at the park. 7 of the children are girls. The rest are boys. How many boys are at the park?

☐ _____
label

3 Georgia has 7 fewer books than her sister. Her sister has 15 books. How many books does Georgia have?

☐ _____
label

4 Jill has 12 stickers. Aspen has 5 stickers. How many fewer stickers does Aspen have than Jill?

☐ _____
label

5 Timothy had 6 markers. Jake gave him some more. Timothy has 11 markers now. How many markers did Jake give Timothy?

☐ _____
label

Name _____

Date _____

Add or subtract.

1 $3 + 0 = \boxed{}$ **2** $5 + 3 = \boxed{}$ **3** $6 + 1 = \boxed{}$

4 $12 - 2 = \boxed{}$ **5** $8 - 2 = \boxed{}$ **6** $14 - 7 = \boxed{}$

7 $9 + 1 = \boxed{}$ **8** $6 + 7 = \boxed{}$ **9** $11 + 9 = \boxed{}$

10
$$\begin{array}{r} 19 \\ -\ 9 \\ \hline \end{array}$$

11
$$\begin{array}{r} 20 \\ -18 \\ \hline \end{array}$$

12
$$\begin{array}{r} 18 \\ -10 \\ \hline \end{array}$$

13
$$\begin{array}{r} 14 \\ +\ 4 \\ \hline \end{array}$$

14
$$\begin{array}{r} 12 \\ +\ 6 \\ \hline \end{array}$$

15
$$\begin{array}{r} 16 \\ +\ 4 \\ \hline \end{array}$$

Complete and Solve Word Problems

Add information so you can solve the problem.
Then solve the problem.

Show your work.

1 Shannon makes a pitcher of lemonade. She uses 8 lemons. How many lemons does she have left?

pitcher

_____

_____

☐ _____
label

2 Sam walks his dog in the morning and again in the afternoon. Altogether Sam and the dog walk 15 blocks. How far do they walk in the morning?

dog

_____

_____

☐ _____
label

3 Kari makes a bracelet with blue and purple beads. 6 beads are blue. How many beads are purple?

beads

_____

_____

☐ _____
label

Solve Problems with Extra Information

VOCABULARY
extra information

Cross out the **extra information**. Solve.

Show your work.

---

④ The dentist has 8 red toothbrushes and 6 green ones. Then she buys 9 more red ones. How many red toothbrushes does she have now?

toothbrush

☐ _____
      label

---

⑤ Rosa has 5 gold coins and 6 silver coins in her collection. Her brother gives her 7 more gold coins. How many gold coins does Rosa have in all?

coin

☐ _____
      label

---

⑥ Pam has 7 long ribbons and 9 short ribbons. She gives away 5 short ones. How many short ribbons does Pam have now?

ribbon

☐ _____
      label

---

⑦ Franny has 8 kittens and 2 dogs. 4 kittens are asleep. How many kittens are awake?

kitten

☐ _____
      label

Problems with Not Enough, Extra, or Hidden Information

Name _____

Find Information in a Story

The Zoo
Today my class went to the zoo. I saw 4 elephants and 5 tigers. The giraffes were tall. There were 8 monkeys playing. I counted 13 penguins. I had fun at the zoo.
By Robbie

Use the story to solve the problems.

Show your work.

---

8 How many more monkeys than tigers did Robbie see?

☐ _____
　　　label

monkey

---

9 How many more penguins than elephants did Robbie see?

☐ _____
　　　label

elephant

---

10 How many fewer tigers than penguins did Robbie see?

☐ _____
　　　label

tiger

Practice Solving Word Problems

Cross out extra information or write missing or **hidden information**. Solve the problem.

VOCABULARY
hidden information

Show your work.

11 Mr. Chris and Mrs. Kelly wash 16 cars at the car wash. How many cars did Mrs. Kelly wash?

car wash

_____

□ _____
  label

12 Kat puts 13 markers and 6 crayons in her book bag. When she gets to school, she gives 4 of the markers to her friend. How many markers does Kat have left?

marker

_____

□ _____
  label

13 There are 9 children and a set of triplets in the library. How many children are in the library?

library

_____

□ _____
  label

 Check Understanding

Will everyone get the same answer to a problem with extra information? How about a problem with missing information? Hidden information?

Problems with Not Enough, Extra, or Hidden Information

Name _____

Solve and Discuss

Draw comparison bars. Write an equation.
Solve the problem.

---

1 Darnell has 6 pens. That is 5 fewer
pens than Natasha. How many pens
does Natasha have?

pen

☐ _____
    label

---

2 There are 7 tigers at the Smithfield Zoo.
The zoo has 9 more lions than tigers.
How many lions does the zoo have?

lion

☐ _____
    label

---

3 Sherean saves $7 more in May than in
April. She saves $15 in May. How many
dollars does she save in April?

dollar

☐ _____
    label

---

4 There are 8 fewer airplane models than
boat models at the craft store. If there
are 9 airplane models, how many boat
models are there?

airplane
model

☐ _____
    label

Content Standards 2.OA.A.1, 2.OA.B.2
Mathematical Practices MP1

Solve and Discuss (continued)

Draw comparison bars. Write an equation.
Solve the problem.

---

5 Chris catches 15 fish. Sean catches
9 fewer fish than Chris. How many
fish does Sean catch?

fish

☐ _____
       label

---

6 There are 9 more apples in the basket
than bananas. There are 17 apples in
the basket. How many bananas are in
the basket?

basket

☐ _____
       label

---

7 There are 5 more horses in the barn
than the field. There are 12 horses in the
barn. How many horses are in the field?

barn

☐ _____
       label

 Check Understanding

Look at Problem 5. What is another way to say
the comparison?

_____

_____

     More Complex *Compare* Problems

Name _____

Model Two-Step Word Problems

Solve the two-step word problem.

Show your work.

---

1 Lindsay brings in 5 cans for the school food drive. Olivia brings in 4 more cans than Lindsay. Matt brings in 6 more cans than Olivia. How many cans does Matt bring?

---

a. How many cans does Olivia bring?

☐ _____
        label

---

b. How many cans does Matt bring?

☐ _____
        label

© Houghton Mifflin Harcourt Publishing Company

Model Two-Step Word Problems (continued)

Solve the two-step word problem.

Show your work.

2 There are 14 computers in the school library. 5 girls and 3 boys are each using a computer right now. How many more children can use a computer?

a. How many children are using computers right now?

☐ _____
    label

b. How many more children can use a computer?

☐ _____
    label

Two-Step Word Problems

Solve Two-Step Word Problems

Think about the first-step question.
Then solve the problem.

Show your work.

3 Mrs. Hadid has 17 tomatoes. She uses
9 tomatoes to make a sauce. Then she
makes a salad with 4 tomatoes. How
many tomatoes does she have left?

tomato

▢ _____

label

4 There are 16 robins in a tree. 9 robins fly away.
Then 4 blue jays fly into the tree. How many
birds are in the tree now?

robin

▢ _____

label

5 Julie has 6 red pencils. She has 2 more
blue pencils than red pencils. How many
pencils does she have in all?

pencil

▢ _____

label

Solve Two-Step Word Problems (continued)

Think about the first-step question.
Then solve the problem.

Show your work.

6 Lana had 9 sheep and some horses on her farm. Altogether there were 17 animals. Her grandmother gives her 3 more horses. How many horses does she have on the farm now?

sheep

☐ _____
  label

7 Rafa has 13 marbles. He has 6 red marbles and the rest are green. Mia gives him some more green marbles. Now Rafa has 12 green marbles. How many green marbles does Mia give Rafa?

marbles

☐ _____
  label

✓ **Check Understanding**

What is the first-step question for Problem 7?

_____

_____

_____

Two-Step Word Problems

Name _____

Solve and Discuss

Make a drawing. Write an equation.
Solve the problem.

Show your work.

1   Mina buys some new shirts. She returns
    4 shirts to the store. Now she has 8 new shirts.
    How many shirts does Mina buy at first?

store

_____
label

2   Marie buys 8 peaches and a dozen apples.
    That is 6 fewer peaches than Rubin buys.
    How many peaches does Rubin buy?

peach

_____
label

3   There are 15 children in the class play.
    9 are boys and the rest are girls.
    Then 3 more girls join the play.
    How many girls are in the play?

children

_____
label

4   Ed buys 9 books at one store and 3 books at
    another. He buys 8 more books than Brenda.
    How many books does Brenda buy?

book

_____
label

Content Standards **2.OA.A.1, 2.OA.B.2**
Mathematical Practices **MP1, MP3, MP4, MP6**

Solve and Discuss (continued)

Make a drawing. Write an equation.
Solve the problem.

Show your work.

⑤ There are some cows in a field. 4 horses join them.
Now there are 12 animals in the field. How many
cows are in the field?

horse

☐ _____
    label

⑥ Rob visits the skate park. He sees 6 skateboards
on Friday, 3 skateboards on Saturday, and
2 skateboards on Sunday. How many skateboards
does Rob see in all?

skateboard

☐ _____
    label

What's the Error?

Felix has 7 white potatoes, 8 purple
potatoes, and 5 green apples. He
uses all the potatoes to make a soup.
How many potatoes does Felix use?

$7 + 8 + 5 = 20$ potatoes
w   p   g

⑦ Help Puzzled Penguin.

✓ **Check Understanding**
Choose one of the problems from this activity and retell it

in your own words. _____

_____

Mixed Word Problems

15 − 6 = ☐   16 − 7 = ☐   11 − 7 = ☐

12 − 8 = ☐   13 − 9 = ☐   11 − 6 = ☐

12 − 7 = ☐   13 − 8 = ☐   14 − 9 = ☐

11 − 5 = ☐   17 − 8 = ☐   13 − 7 = ☐

14 − 8 = ☐   15 − 9 = ☐   11 − 4 = ☐

$$11 - 7 = \boxed{4}$$
3
1

$$16 - 7 = \boxed{9}$$
3
6

$$15 - 6 = \boxed{9}$$
4
5

$$11 - 6 = \boxed{5}$$
4
1

$$13 - 9 = \boxed{4}$$
1
3

$$12 - 8 = \boxed{4}$$
2
2

$$14 - 9 = \boxed{5}$$
1
4

$$13 - 8 = \boxed{5}$$
2
3

$$12 - 7 = \boxed{5}$$
3
2

$$13 - 7 = \boxed{6}$$
3
3

$$17 - 8 = \boxed{9}$$
2
7

$$11 - 5 = \boxed{6}$$
5
1

$$11 - 4 = \boxed{7}$$
6
1

$$15 - 9 = \boxed{6}$$
1
5

$$14 - 8 = \boxed{6}$$
2
4

Blue Make-a-Ten Cards

$12 - 5 = \boxed{}$ $13 - 6 = \boxed{}$ $18 - 9 = \boxed{}$

$15 - 8 = \boxed{}$ $16 - 9 = \boxed{}$ $11 - 3 = \boxed{}$

$12 - 4 = \boxed{}$ $13 - 5 = \boxed{}$ $14 - 6 = \boxed{}$

$15 - 7 = \boxed{}$ $16 - 8 = \boxed{}$ $17 - 9 = \boxed{}$

$12 - 3 = \boxed{}$ $13 - 4 = \boxed{}$ $14 - 5 = \boxed{}$

$$18 - 9 = \boxed{9}$$
1
8

$$13 - 6 = \boxed{7}$$
4
3

$$12 - 5 = \boxed{7}$$
5
2

$$11 - 3 = \boxed{8}$$
7
1

$$16 - 9 = \boxed{7}$$
1
6

$$15 - 8 = \boxed{7}$$
2
5

$$14 - 6 = \boxed{8}$$
4
4

$$13 - 5 = \boxed{8}$$
5
3

$$12 - 4 = \boxed{8}$$
6
2

$$17 - 9 = \boxed{8}$$
1
7

$$16 - 8 = \boxed{8}$$
2
6

$$15 - 7 = \boxed{8}$$
3
5

$$14 - 5 = \boxed{9}$$
5
4

$$13 - 4 = \boxed{9}$$
6
3

$$12 - 3 = \boxed{9}$$
7
2

Blue Make-a-Ten Cards

Name _____

Solve Problems and Compare Methods

Beren and her friends are making funny face pizzas.

1 Darryl uses 2 green olives for eyes and 9 black olives to make a big smile. How many olives does he use?

☐ _____
label

2 Sarah uses 6 fewer mushroom slices than Darryl. Sarah uses 8 slices. How many slices of mushroom does Darryl use?

☐ _____
label

3 When they start making the pizzas, there are a dozen small tomatoes. Darryl uses 2 tomatoes. Beren and Dawn each use 1 tomato. No one else uses any. How many tomatoes are left?

☐ _____
label

CCSS Content Standards **2.OA.A.1, 2.OA.B.2**
Mathematical Practices **MP1, MP3, MP4, MP5, MP6**

Problems with Extra Information

Solve. Cross out the information you do not need.   **Show your work.**

④ Beren makes a fruit salad. She uses 2 strawberries,
8 blueberries, 7 raspberries, and 3 apples.
How many berries does she use?

☐ _____
　　　　label

⑤ Darryl makes a snack mix. He uses 2 cups of
cereal, 4 cups of raisins, 3 cups of dried cherries,
and 2 cups of walnuts. How many more cups of
dried fruit does he use than cups of nuts?

☐ _____
　　　　label

Write and Solve a Problem

"Ants on a Log" is a snack made with celery, peanut
butter, and raisins.

Beren's Snack　　**Darryl's Snack**　　**Sarah's Snack**

⑥ Use the pictures. On a separate sheet of paper,
write a problem.

Exchange with a classmate. Solve each other's
problem.

Focus on Mathematical Practices

1. Add more information so you can solve the problem. Solve.

   Kelly makes banana bread. She uses 2 bananas. How many bananas does she have left?

   _____

2. Write the hidden information. Then solve.

   There are 8 children and a set of young twins at the park. How many children are at the park?

   _____

Solve.   **Show your work.**

3. Mrs. Green had 7 science books and 5 history books. Then she bought 8 more science books. How many science books does she have now?

   ☐ _____
       label

4. Nancy picks 17 apples. Pete picks 9 fewer apples than Nancy. How many apples does Pete pick?

   ☐ _____
       label

5. Abdul had 14 cards. He had 8 baseball cards and the rest were football cards. Jason gives Abdul some more football cards. Now Abdul has 13 football cards. How many football cards does Jason give Abdul?

   ☐ _____
       label

Name _____   **Date** _____

Add or subtract.

1 $16 - 8 = \boxed{}$ **2** $11 - 2 = \boxed{}$ **3** $5 - 2 = \boxed{}$

4 $6 + 5 = \boxed{}$ **5** $2 + 0 = \boxed{}$ **6** $7 + 4 = \boxed{}$

7
$$\begin{array}{r} 13 \\ -\ 6 \\ \hline \end{array}$$

8
$$\begin{array}{r} 16 \\ -\ 9 \\ \hline \end{array}$$

9
$$\begin{array}{r} 13 \\ -\ 5 \\ \hline \end{array}$$

10
$$\begin{array}{r} 14 \\ +\ 6 \\ \hline \end{array}$$

11
$$\begin{array}{r} 10 \\ +\ 8 \\ \hline \end{array}$$

12
$$\begin{array}{r} 12 \\ +\ 7 \\ \hline \end{array}$$

13
$$\begin{array}{r} 17 \\ -16 \\ \hline \end{array}$$

14
$$\begin{array}{r} 19 \\ -15 \\ \hline \end{array}$$

15
$$\begin{array}{r} 20 \\ -16 \\ \hline \end{array}$$

Write each addition or subtraction in the box below
the correct answer.

① $0 + 7$ $7 + 7$ $12 - 5$ $20 - 6$ $13 - 1$

7	12	14

Write the partner or total in the box.

② $5 + 0 = \boxed{}$ ③ $15 - 6 = \boxed{}$

④ $\boxed{} = 3 + 8$ ⑤ $3 + 4 + 6 = \boxed{}$

⑥ $7 + 9 = \boxed{}$ ⑦ $15 - 8 = \boxed{}$

---

⑧ Is the total 12? Choose Yes or No.

$5 + 6$	○ Yes	○ No
$7 + 5$	○ Yes	○ No
$12 + 0$	○ Yes	○ No
$4 + 9$	○ Yes	○ No
$2 + 10$	○ Yes	○ No

9 Complete the Math Mountain.

Write an addition and a subtraction
equation to go with it.

_____

_____

How are the equations related?

_____

_____

Solve.

10 Beth has a bag of apples. She gives 3 apples
to Natasha. Now she has 15 apples left.
How many apples were in the bag at first?

⬜ _____
　　label

11 Evan finds 12 shells. Aaron finds 5 fewer shells
than Evan. How many shells does Aaron find?

⬜ _____
　　label

12 Make a drawing. Write an equation.
    Solve the problem.

    Linda sees 18 cows and 12 horses in a field.
    There are 8 brown cows. The rest are white.
    How many cows are white?

    ☐ _____
           label

---

13 Choose an even number. Write a doubles addition
    equation with your number. Explain how you know
    the total is even.

    _____

    _____

---

14 Match each addition or subtraction to the correct answer.

    $2 + 4 + 6$ •   • 9

    $16 - 8$ •   • 12

    $13 + 7$ •   • 20

    $14 - 5$ •   • 8

Solve. Circle the correct answer.

15 There are some frogs on a rock.
Then 9 more frogs jump on the rock.
Now there are 14 frogs.
How many frogs were on the rock at first?

There were
| 5 |
| 6 |
| 13 |
frogs on the rock at first.

---

16 There are 6 basketballs, 3 footballs, and 9 baseballs on the playground. How many balls are on the playground?

There are
| 16 |
| 18 |
| 19 |
balls on the playground.

Draw comparison bars. Write an equation.
Solve the problem.

17 Madison has 11 grapes in a bowl.
Hailey has 5 more grapes than Madison.
How many grapes does Hailey have?

☐ _____
    label

At the Pond

Choose any method to solve the problem.   **Show your work.**

1 3 ducks are in the pond. Then 6 more ducks
jump in the pond. Later, 7 more ducks jump in.
How many ducks are in the pond now?

☐ _____
        label

2 Choose one of these numbers for each ◯.

3   7

There are 16 turtles sitting near the pond.

◯ turtles went away.

How many turtles are left?

☐ _____
        label

◯ more turtles went away.

How many turtles are left?

☐ _____
        label

3 Did you use a different method when you
subtracted 7 than when you subtracted 3? Explain.

_____

_____

_____

4 Sonia and Amy each collected leaves at the pond.
Together they collected 19 leaves.

How many leaves did each girl collect?
Write 3 different possible answers.

_____ and _____
    Sonia   Amy

OR

_____ and _____
    Sonia   Amy

OR

_____ and _____
    Sonia   Amy

5 Pick one of the ways you showed above.
Complete the equation to show how many more
leaves one girl collected than the other girl.

_____ − _____ = _____

Make a drawing to show your equation is correct.

© Houghton Mifflin Harcourt Publishing Company

Dear Family:

Your child is learning about place value and will use this knowledge to add 2- and 3-digit numbers.

As we begin this unit, your child will represent numbers using drawings like this one:

Then, children will begin to represent numbers using Quick Hundreds and Quick Tens.

Name a 2- or 3-digit number and ask your child to make a drawing to represent that number.

Later in this unit, children will work on adding 2-digit numbers using the drawings to help them.

Thank you. Please contact me if you have any questions.

Sincerely,
Your child's teacher

CC SS Unit 2 addresses the following standards from the Common Core State Standards for Mathematics: **2.OA.A.1, 2.OA.B.2, 2.NBT.A.1, 2.NBT.A.1.a, 2.NBT.A.2, 2.NBT.A.3, 2.NBT.A.4, 2.NBT.B.5, 2.NBT.B.6, 2.NBT.B.7, 2.NBT.B.8, 2.NBT.B.9, 2.MD.C.8**, and all Mathematical Practices.

Estimada familia:

Su niño está aprendiendo acerca del valor posicional y usará esos conocimientos para sumar números de 2 y 3 dígitos.

Cuando comencemos con esta unidad, su niño representará números usando dibujos como este:

Luego, los niños comenzarán a representar números usando "Centenas rápidas" y "Decenas rápidas".

Centena rápida	Decenas rápidas	Unidades

146

100   +   40   +   6

Diga un número de 2 ó 3 dígitos y pida a su niño que haga un dibujo para representar ese número.

Más adelante, los niños trabajarán sumando números de 2 dígitos y usarán los dibujos como ayuda.

Gracias. Si tiene alguna pregunta, por favor comuníquese conmigo.

Atentamente,
El maestro de su niño

© Houghton Mifflin Harcourt Publishing Company

En la Unidad 2 se aplican los siguientes estándares de los Estándares estatales comunes de matemáticas: **2.OA.A.1, 2.OA.B.2, 2.NBT.A.1, 2.NBT.A.1.a, 2.NBT.A.2, 2.NBT.A.3, 2.NBT.A.4, 2.NBT.B.5, 2.NBT.B.6, 2.NBT.B.7, 2.NBT.B.8, 2.NBT.B.9, 2.MD.C.8 y todos los de** Prácticas matemáticas.

Ones, Tens, and Hundreds

expanded form

is less than (<)

is equal to (=)

number name

is greater than (>)

||||°°°°° ||||°°°°°
          °

45   <   **46**

45 is less than 46.

$$283 = 200 + 80 + 3$$

12

twelve ←—— number name

$$5 + 3 = 8$$

5 plus 3 is equal to 8.

|||°°°° ||°°°°°

34   >   **25**

34 is greater than 25.

Name _____

Write the Numbers 101 to 200

1 Write the numbers going down to see the tens.

101	111								
102		122			152				
103						163			193
				144					
								185	
	116				156				
		128							
								189	
110	120			150		170			200

CC SS Content Standards **2.OA.A.1, 2.NBT.A.1, 2.NBT.A.2, 2.NBT.A.3**
Mathematical Practices **MP1, MP4, MP7**

Word Problem Practice: Addition and Subtraction Within 20

Solve.   **Show your work.**

---

2 Sara has some marbles. Shane gives her 8 more marbles. Now Sara has 17 marbles. How many marbles did Sara have at first?

marbles

☐ _____
    label

---

3 There are 14 children on the soccer field. There are 8 boys, and the rest are girls. Then 2 girls leave the soccer field. How many girls are on the soccer field now?

soccer field

☐ _____
    label

---

4 In the lunchroom, 16 children have apples. 9 of these children have red apples, and the rest have green apples. Then 5 more children come with green apples. How many children have green apples now?

apple

☐ _____
    label

✓ **Check Understanding**
Describe the number 106 in two different ways.

© Houghton Mifflin Harcourt Publishing Company

1	2	10	20
1	2	1 0	2 0

3	4	30	40
3	4	3 0	4 0

5	6	50	60
5	6	5 0	6 0

7	8	70	80
7	8	7 0	8 0

9	90	100
9	9 0	1 0 0

Secret Code Cards (1–100) **89**

Secret Code Cards (1–100)

Name _____

Add Tens or Ones

Add.

① 10 + 20 = _____   70 + 20 = _____   60 + 30 = _____

   1 + 2 = _____   7 + 2 = _____   6 + 3 = _____

② 20 + 70 = _____   30 + 50 = _____   40 + 50 = _____

   2 + 7 = _____   3 + 5 = _____   4 + 5 = _____

③ 30 + 60 = _____   20 + 80 = _____   50 + 40 = _____

   3 + 6 = _____   2 + 8 = _____   5 + 4 = _____

④ 50 + 50 = _____   80 + 20 = _____   40 + 60 = _____

   5 + 5 = _____   8 + 2 = _____   4 + 6 = _____

⑤ 90 + 10 = _____   90 + 20 = _____   40 + 30 = _____

   9 + 1 = _____   9 + 2 = _____   4 + 3 = _____

⑥ 50 + 20 = _____   20 + 30 = _____   60 + 70 = _____

   5 + 2 = _____   2 + 3 = _____   6 + 7 = _____

Content Standards 2.OA.A.1, 2.OA.B.2, 2.NBT.A.3, 2.NBT.B.5, 2.NBT.B.9
Mathematical Practices MP7

Word Problem Practice: Addition and Subtraction Within 20

Solve. **Show your work.**

---

7 Some crayons are on the table.
Mrs. Spain takes 5 of the crayons.
Now there are 8 crayons on the table.
How many crayons were on the table before?

crayon

☐ _____
label

---

8 The jewelry store has 8 red bracelets and some
blue bracelets. There are 15 bracelets in all.
Then 3 blue bracelets are sold. How many blue
bracelets are still in the store?

bracelet

☐ _____
label

---

9 Mr. Rivera bakes 7 banana muffins and 9 orange
muffins. He gives some muffins to his friends. Now
he has 8 muffins. How many muffins does he give
to his friends?

muffin

☐ _____
label

 Check Understanding
Draw Quick Tens and circles to represent 79.

Draw Quick Tens and Quick Hundreds

Name _____

Hundreds, Tens, and Ones

Draw the number using boxes, 10-sticks, and circles.
Then write the **expanded form**.

①
⭘⭘⭘⭘⭘
⭘

106

_100_ + _0_ + _6_

②

122

___ + ___ + ___

③

139

___ + ___ + ___

What number is shown?   H = Hundreds, T = Tens, O = Ones

④

⭘⭘⭘⭘⭘
⭘⭘

_1_ H _4_ T _7_ O

_147_ = _100_ + _40_ + _7_

⑤

⭘

___ H ___ T ___ O

___ = ___ + ___ + ___

⑥

___ H ___ T ___ O

___ = ___ + ___ + ___

⑦

⭘⭘⭘⭘⭘
⭘⭘⭘⭘

___ H ___ T ___ O

___ = ___ + ___ + ___

Content Standards **2.NBT.A.1, 2.NBT.A.2, 2.NBT.A.3**
Mathematical Practices **MP7**

Represent Numbers in Different Ways **93**

Read and Write Number Names

VOCABULARY
number name

1 one	11 eleven	10 ten	100 one hundred
2 two	12 twelve	20 twenty	
3 three	13 thirteen	30 thirty	
4 four	14 fourteen	40 forty	
5 five	15 fifteen	50 fifty	
6 six	16 sixteen	60 sixty	
7 seven	17 seventeen	70 seventy	
8 eight	18 eighteen	80 eighty	
9 nine	19 nineteen	90 ninety	

Write the number.

8 thirty-five _____

9 seventy-two _____

10 fifty-four _____

11 eighty-nine _____

Write the number name.

12 47 _____

13 62 _____

14 85 _____

15 94 _____

Represent Write the number name, then draw Quick Tens and ones in the box.

16 60 _____

17 72 _____

© Houghton Mifflin Harcourt Publishing Company

 Check Understanding
Explain how to represent 132 in expanded form.

Represent Numbers in Different Ways

Name _____

Word Problems with Groups of Ten

Solve. Make a proof drawing.

① Remah has 34 stickers. Only 10 stickers fit on a page in her sticker book. How many pages can she fill with stickers? How many stickers will be left over?

[ ] pages   [ ] stickers left over

② David has 42 beads. He wants to make some necklaces that use 10 beads each. How many necklaces can he make? How many beads will be left over?

[ ] necklaces   [ ] beads left over

③ The team wants to buy T-shirts that cost 10 dollars each. They have 57 dollars. How many T-shirts can they buy? How many dollars will be left over?

[ ] T-shirts   [ ] dollars left over

④ There are 163 apples at the fruit stand. Each basket can hold 10 apples. How many baskets can be filled with apples? How many apples will be left over?

[ ] baskets   [ ] apples left over

Add 1, 10, or 100

Add.

⑤ $38 + 1 =$ _____

⑥ $9 + 10 =$ _____

⑦ $24 + 100 =$ _____

⑧ $150 + 1 =$ _____

⑨ $7 + 100 =$ _____

⑩ $92 + 10 =$ _____

⑪ $59 + 1 =$ _____

⑫ $166 + 10 =$ _____

⑬ $10 + 10 =$ _____

⑭ $143 + 1 =$ _____

⑮ $98 + 100 =$ _____

⑯ $46 + 10 =$ _____

⑰ $11 + 100 =$ _____

⑱ $195 + 1 =$ _____

⑲ $104 + 10 =$ _____

⑳ $30 + 100 =$ _____

✔ **Check Understanding**

Draw to show how to find the total for $58 + 10$.

Combine Ones, Tens, and Hundreds

Name _____

VOCABULARY
is less than (<)
is greater than (>)
is equal to (=)

Use Drawings to Compare Numbers

Use these symbols to compare numbers.

< is less than   > is greater than   = is equal to

Make a drawing for each number. Write <, >, or =.

1 56 ◯ 81   **2** 123 ◯ 109

3 101 ◯ 101   **4** 98 ◯ 150

5 67 ◯ 76   **6** 120 ◯ 102

CCSS Content Standards **2.NBT.A.1, 2.NBT.A.3, 2.NBT.A.4**
Mathematical Practices **MP2, MP3, MP6, MP8**

Compare Numbers

Write <, >, or =.

7 135 ◯ 137

8 83 ◯ 83

9 119 ◯ 87

10 127 ◯ 172

11 62 ◯ 57

12 51 ◯ 15

13 111 ◯ 111

14 37 ◯ 74

15 192 ◯ 191

16 100 ◯ 10

What's the Error?

149 (>) 176

I know that 9 is greater than 6. Did I make a mistake?

17 Make a proof drawing to help Puzzled Penguin.
Write <, >, or =.

149 ◯ 176

✔ **Check Understanding**

When comparing two 3-digit numbers, which place value position should be compared first? Circle your answer.

hundreds   tens   ones

Compare Numbers Within 200

Name_____ Date_____

Write the correct answer.

1 What number is shown? Write the number.

_____

---

2 Draw the number using hundred boxes, 10-sticks, and circles. Then write the number in expanded form.

131

_____

---

3 What number is shown?
Write the number and the number name.

_____

_____

---

4 Add.

100 + 5 = ☐

---

5 Compare. Write >, <, or =.

126 ◯ 136

Name _____ **Date** _____

Add or subtract.

1 $5 + 1 =$ ☐   **2** $7 + 5 =$ ☐   **3** $4 + 4 =$ ☐

4 $13 - 3 =$ ☐   **5** $8 - 2 =$ ☐   **6** $16 - 8 =$ ☐

7 $9 + 4 =$ ☐   **8** $8 + 4 =$ ☐   **9** $7 + 8 =$ ☐

10
$$\begin{array}{r} 17 \\ -11 \\ \hline \end{array}$$

11
$$\begin{array}{r} 20 \\ -\ 4 \\ \hline \end{array}$$

12
$$\begin{array}{r} 19 \\ -\ 7 \\ \hline \end{array}$$

13
$$\begin{array}{r} 9 \\ +\ 9 \\ \hline \end{array}$$

14
$$\begin{array}{r} 8 \\ +\ 9 \\ \hline \end{array}$$

15
$$\begin{array}{r} 10 \\ +10 \\ \hline \end{array}$$

Dear Family:

Your child is now learning how to add 2-digit numbers. The "big mystery" in adding is making a new ten or a new hundred. Children can write this new group in several ways.

Show All Totals	New Groups Below
$$\begin{array}{r} 45 \\ +\ 28 \\ \hline \end{array}$$ Add tens. → 60 Add ones. → 13 $$\hline$$ 73 Find total tens. Find total ones. New ten	$$\begin{array}{r} 45 \\ +\ 28 \\ \hline 73 \end{array}$$ New ten Find total ones. (13) Write 3 and put the new ten in the tens column, ready to add. Add the tens. (4 + 2 = 6, 6 + 1 = 7)

New Groups Above

$$\begin{array}{r} 1 \\ 45 \\ +\ 28 \\ \hline 73 \end{array}$$

Children usually find it easier to write the new ten below because then they add the new ten last. They add 4 + 2 = 6 and then 6 + 1 = 7.

Traditionally, most children have learned to write the new ten above. With this method, you add 1 + 4 = 5 and then 5 + 2 = 7. This is more difficult for many children, but some children may still choose this method, particularly if they have been taught to do so previously.

Thank you for helping your child learn mathematics.

Sincerely,
Your child's teacher

CC SS Unit 2 addresses the following standards from the Common Core State Standards for Mathematics: **2.OA.A.1, 2.OA.B.2, 2.NBT.A.1, 2.NBT.A.1.a, 2.NBT.A.2, 2.NBT.A.3, 2.NBT.A.4, 2.NBT.B.5, 2.NBT.B.6, 2.NBT.B.7, 2.NBT.B.8, 2.NBT.B.9, 2.MD.C.8, and all** Mathematical Practices.

Estimada familia:

Su niño está aprendiendo a sumar números de 2 dígitos. El "gran misterio" en la suma de números de 2 dígitos consiste en formar una nueva decena o una nueva centena. Los niños pueden anotar este nuevo grupo de varias maneras.

Mostrar todos los totales	Grupos nuevos abajo

Mostrar todos los totales:

$$45$$
$$+\,28$$
Sumar decenas. → 60
Sumar unidades. → 13
$$73$$

Nueva decena

Hallar el total de decenas.   Hallar el total de unidades.

Grupos nuevos abajo:

$$45$$
$$+\,28$$
$$73$$

Nueva decena

Hallar el total de unidades. (13) Escribir 3 y poner la nueva decena en la columna de las decenas, lista para sumar.

Sumar las decenas. (4 + 2 = 6, 6 + 1 = 7)

Grupos nuevos arriba

$$1$$
$$45$$
$$+\,28$$
$$73$$

Por lo general a los niños les resulta más fácil escribir la nueva decena abajo, porque entonces suman la nueva decena al final. Suman 4 + 2 = 6 y luego 6 + 1 = 7.

Tradicionalmente, la mayoría de los estudiantes han aprendido a escribir la nueva decena arriba. Con ese método, se suma 1 + 4 = 5 y luego 5 + 2 = 7. Para muchos niños ese método resulta más difícil pero algunos siguen escogiéndolo, en especial si ya lo han aprendido.

Gracias por ayudar a su niño a aprender matemáticas.

Atentamente,
El maestro de su niño

En la Unidad 2 se aplican los siguientes estándares de los Estándares estatales comunes de matemáticas: **2.OA.A.1, 2.OA.B.2, 2.NBT.A.1, 2.NBT.A.1.a, 2.NBT.A.2, 2.NBT.A.3, 2.NBT.A.4, 2.NBT.B.5, 2.NBT.B.6, 2.NBT.B.7, 2.NBT.B.8, 2.NBT.B.9, 2.MD.C.8 y todos los de** Prácticas matemáticas.

Explore 2-Digit Addition

Name _____

The New Ten

Solve each word problem.

Show your work.

1 Mr. Green puts 56 red peppers in the
   vegetable bin. Mrs. Green puts 28 yellow
   peppers in the bin. How many peppers
   do they put in the bin altogether?

   ☐ _____
   label

2 Mrs. Green stacks 43 tomatoes.
   Mr. Green adds 39 more.
   How many tomatoes do they stack in all?

   ☐ _____
   label

The New Hundred

3 Mr. Green counts 65 cans.
   Mrs. Green counts 82 cans.
   How many cans do they count in all?

   ☐ _____
   label

4 Mrs. Green counts 57 bags of beans.
   Mr. Green counts 71 bags of beans.
   How many bags of beans do they count in all?

   ☐ _____
   label

Content Standards 2.OA.A.1, 2.OA.B.2, 2.NBT.A.1, 2.NBT.A.1.a, 2.NBT.B.6, 2.NBT.B.9
Mathematical Practices MP1, MP4, MP7

Explore 2-Digit Addition **103**

Make a Ten or Hundred

Solve each word problem.

Show your work.

⑤ Mrs. Green stacks 37 boxes of mushrooms.
Mr. Green stacks 29 boxes of mushrooms.
How many boxes do they stack altogether?

[   ] _____
      label

⑥ Mr. Green sells 65 bananas.
Mrs. Green sells 54 bananas.
How many bananas do they sell in all?

[   ] _____
      label

(PATH to FLUENCY) **Add and Subtract Within 20**

Add or subtract.

⑦ $6 + 8 =$ _____

⑧ $9 + 7 =$ _____

⑨ $6 + 10 =$ _____

⑩ $\begin{array}{r} 9 \\ + 4 \\ \hline \end{array}$

⑪ $\begin{array}{r} 10 \\ + 1 \\ \hline \end{array}$

⑫ $\begin{array}{r} 7 \\ + 6 \\ \hline \end{array}$

⑬ $15 - 7 =$ _____

⑭ $20 - 10 =$ _____

⑮ $18 - 9 =$ _____

⑯ $\begin{array}{r} 11 \\ - 6 \\ \hline \end{array}$

⑰ $\begin{array}{r} 15 \\ - 8 \\ \hline \end{array}$

⑱ $\begin{array}{r} 16 \\ - 7 \\ \hline \end{array}$

✔ **Check Understanding**

Make a proof drawing to represent how you would add $67 + 41$.

© Houghton Mifflin Harcourt Publishing Company

Explore 2-Digit Addition

Name _____

Show All Totals Method

Solve. Make a proof drawing.

Show your work.

1. Mr. Green orders 25 jars of grape jelly and 48 jars of strawberry jelly. How many jars of jelly does he order?

[   ] _____
          label

2. On Monday, Mrs. Green orders 65 pounds of bananas. On Thursday, she orders 29 more pounds of bananas. How many pounds of bananas does she order altogether?

[   ] _____
          label

3. Mrs. Green orders 78 pounds of white rice and 57 pounds of brown rice. How many pounds of rice does she order?

[   ] _____
          label

4. Mr. Green orders 49 jars of plain peanut butter and 86 jars of chunky peanut butter. How many jars of peanut butter does he order in all?

[   ] _____
          label

Word Problem Practice: Two-Step Word Problems

Solve.   **Show your work.**

5️⃣ There were 17 plums on the table. Nine plums were sold. Mr. Green puts some more plums on the table. Now there are 13 plums. How many plums did Mr. Green put on the table?

plum

⬜ _____
label

6️⃣ Some carrots are in a basket. Fran adds 5 more carrots to the basket. James places 4 more carrots there. Now there are 13 carrots. How many carrots were in the basket in the beginning?

carrots

⬜ _____
label

7️⃣ Jane buys 8 bananas. Damon buys 4 fewer bananas than Jane. How many bananas do they buy in all?

bananas

⬜ _____
label

 Check Understanding

Describe how the Show All Totals method could be used to add 82 + 45.

Addition—Show All Totals Method

Name _____

Add with New Groups Below

$$\begin{array}{r} 47 \\ + 65 \\ \hline 112 \end{array}$$

Use the New Groups Below method to add.
Make a proof drawing.

1
$$\begin{array}{r} 31 \\ + 49 \\ \hline \end{array}$$
$$\begin{array}{r} 76 \\ + 52 \\ \hline \end{array}$$

2
$$\begin{array}{r} 78 \\ + 18 \\ \hline \end{array}$$
$$\begin{array}{r} 67 \\ + 69 \\ \hline \end{array}$$

3
$$\begin{array}{r} 26 \\ + 78 \\ \hline \end{array}$$
$$\begin{array}{r} 46 \\ + 84 \\ \hline \end{array}$$

Content Standards 2.OA.A.1, 2.NBT.A.1, 2.NBT.A.1.a, 2.NBT.B.6, 2.NBT.B.7, 2.NBT.B.9 **Mathematical Practices** MP1, MP3, MP6

Addition—New Groups Below Method **107**

Add with New Groups Below (continued)

Use the New Groups Below method to add.
Make a proof drawing.

4
$$\begin{array}{r} 72 \\ + 54 \\ \hline \end{array}$$
$$\begin{array}{r} 13 \\ + 26 \\ \hline \end{array}$$

What do you notice about the new groups in these two problems? Explain how the problems are different.

_____

_____

_____

Solve Word Problems with New Groups Below

Read the problem. Write the addition problem in vertical form. Solve it using the New Groups Below method.

5 Kat helped her uncle pull weeds in the garden. Kat pulled 90 weeds. Her uncle pulled 15 weeds. How many weeds did they pull in all?

_____ weeds

6 Gia's dress has 17 red polka dots and 34 blue polka dots. How many polka dots are on Gia's dress?

_____ polka dots

 Check Understanding

Explain how to add 25 + 75 using the New Groups Below method.

Addition—New Groups Below Method

Name _____

Practice and Share

Add. Use any method.

$$
\begin{array}{r}
86 \\
+\ 57 \\
\hline
130 \\
+\ 13 \\
\hline
143
\end{array}
\quad \text{or} \quad
\begin{array}{r}
86 \\
+\ 57 \\
\hline
143
\end{array}
$$

$$130 + 13 = 143$$

1
$$
\begin{array}{r}
39 \\
+\ 97 \\
\hline
\end{array}
\qquad\qquad
\begin{array}{r}
83 \\
+\ 39 \\
\hline
\end{array}
$$

2
$$
\begin{array}{r}
58 \\
+\ 87 \\
\hline
\end{array}
\qquad\qquad
\begin{array}{r}
72 \\
+\ 37 \\
\hline
\end{array}
$$

3
$$
\begin{array}{r}
49 \\
+\ 85 \\
\hline
\end{array}
\qquad\qquad
\begin{array}{r}
94 \\
+\ 52 \\
\hline
\end{array}
$$

CC SS Content Standards 2.NBT.A.1, 2.NBT.A.1.a, 2.NBT.B.6, 2.NBT.B.7, 2.NBT.B.9
Mathematical Practices MP1, MP2, MP3, MP6

Predict a New Ten or New Hundred

Add. Use any method.

④
```
  61
+ 37
```

```
  53
+ 98
```

⑤
```
  42
+ 80
```

```
  66
+ 27
```

What's the Error?

```
  38
+ 46
----
  74
```

I know that 3 tens plus 4 tens equals 7 tens. Did I make a mistake?

⑥ Show Puzzled Penguin how you would add the numbers.
Make a proof drawing to check your work.

```
  38
+ 46
```

✓ Check Understanding

Find the sum of 76 + 25. Which did you make?
Circle your answer.

new ten   both

new hundred   neither

© Houghton Mifflin Harcourt Publishing Company

Practice Addition with Sums Over 100

What's the Error?

$$
\begin{array}{r}
32 \\
+\ 25 \\
\hline
67
\end{array}
$$

Did I make a mistake?

1 Add. Make a proof drawing.

$$
\begin{array}{r}
32 \\
+\ 25 \\
\hline
\end{array}
$$

$$
\begin{array}{r}
48 \\
+\ 43 \\
\hline
811
\end{array}
$$

Is this correct?

2 Add. Make a proof drawing.

$$
\begin{array}{r}
48 \\
+\ 43 \\
\hline
\end{array}
$$

CC SS Content Standards 2.NBT.A.1, 2.NBT.B.6, 2.NBT.B.7, 2.NBT.B.9
Mathematical Practices MP3, MP6

What's the Error? (continued)

$$\begin{array}{r} \overset{1}{1}7 \\ +\ 66 \\ \hline 74 \end{array}$$

Is this one correct?

3 Add. Make a proof drawing.

$$\begin{array}{r} 17 \\ +\ 66 \\ \hline \end{array}$$

$$\begin{array}{r} \overset{3}{3}9 \\ +\ 54 \\ \hline 111 \end{array}$$

Did I add correctly this time?

4 Add. Make a proof drawing.

$$\begin{array}{r} 39 \\ +\ 54 \\ \hline \end{array}$$

Choose a Method

Add. Use any method.

5
$$\begin{array}{r} 73 \\ +\ 42 \\ \hline \end{array} \qquad \begin{array}{r} 26 \\ +\ 85 \\ \hline \end{array} \qquad \begin{array}{r} 58 \\ +\ 34 \\ \hline \end{array}$$

✓ Check Understanding

Which method did Puzzled Penguin use in Exercise 4?

Choose an Addition Method

Add.

① 64
+ 27

② 86
+ 59

Solve each word problem.

Show your work.

③ Wyatt has 16 stickers. Henry has 17 stickers.
How many stickers do they have in all?

[ ] _____
        label

④ Erika has 74 shells. Ian has 58 shells.
How many shells do they have in all?

[ ] _____
        label

⑤ A pet store has 11 blue birds and 18 yellow birds.
How many birds does the store have in all?

[ ] _____
        label

Name _____   **Date** _____

Add or subtract.

1 $9 - 4 = \boxed{}$ **2** $17 - 3 = \boxed{}$ **3** $8 - 8 = \boxed{}$

4 $7 + 4 = \boxed{}$ **5** $2 + 3 = \boxed{}$ **6** $6 + 6 = \boxed{}$

7 $16 - 15 = \boxed{}$ **8** $15 - 9 = \boxed{}$ **9** $16 - 9 = \boxed{}$

10 $\begin{array}{r} 7 \\ + 9 \\ \hline \end{array}$ **11** $\begin{array}{r} 10 \\ + 9 \\ \hline \end{array}$ **12** $\begin{array}{r} 10 \\ + 8 \\ \hline \end{array}$

13 $\begin{array}{r} 19 \\ - 9 \\ \hline \end{array}$ **14** $\begin{array}{r} 18 \\ - 5 \\ \hline \end{array}$ **15** $\begin{array}{r} 20 \\ - 11 \\ \hline \end{array}$

Cut along the dashed lines.

Dollar Bills

Dollar Bills

Name _____

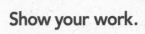

Find the Amount

Write the answer using ¢.
Then write the answer using $.

Show your work.

_____

1. Joe has 11 dimes and 4 pennies.
   How much money does Joe have?

   _____   _____

2. Devin has 1 dollar, 3 dimes, and 8 pennies.
   How much money does Devin have?

   _____   _____

3. Forrest has 14 dimes and 15 pennies.
   How much money does Forrest have?

   _____   _____

4. Kasey has 2 dimes, 6 pennies, and 1 dollar.
   How much money does Kasey have?

   _____   _____

5. Carlito has 1 dollar, 8 dimes, and 19 pennies.
   How much money does Carlito have?

   _____   _____

The Farm Stand

Potatoes 65¢	Corn 56¢	Bananas 89¢	Peaches 77¢
Radishes 76¢	Lemons 88¢	Celery 57¢	Peppers 78¢
Mushrooms 67¢	Carrots 86¢	Tomatoes 97¢	Grapes 98¢
Watermelon 59¢	Oranges 85¢	Raspberries 99¢	Green Beans 87¢

✔ **Check Understanding**

Explain how to find the sum of 67¢ and 45¢.

© Houghton Mifflin Harcourt Publishing Company

Buy with Pennies and Dimes

Name _____

Practice Counting by 5s

1 Go across. Loop groups of 5 jars. Write the numbers.

1	2	3	4		6	7	8	9	
11	12	13	14		16	17	18	19	
21	22	23	24		26	27	28	29	
31	32	33	34		36	37	38	39	
41	42	43	44		46	47	48	49	
51	52	53	54		56	57	58	59	
61	62	63	64		66	67	68	69	
71	72	73	74		76	77	78	79	
81	82	83	84		86	87	88	89	
91	92	93	94		96	97	98	99	

CC SS Content Standards 2.NBT.A.2, 2.MD.C.8
Mathematical Practices MP3, MP4, MP6, MP7

Pennies, Nickels, and Dimes **119**

How Many Cents?

Under the coins, write the total amount of money so far.
Then write the total using $. The first one is done for you.

2

5¢   5¢   5¢

_5¢_   _10¢_   _15¢_ $ _0_ . _1_ _5_

total

3

5¢   5¢   5¢   5¢

____ ____ ____ ____ $ __ . __ __

total

4

5¢   5¢   5¢   5¢   5¢

____ ____ ____ ____ ____ $ __ . __ __

total

5 Pedro has 9 nickels. Draw (5)s to show his nickels.

Write the total amount of money. $ __ . __ __

total

Pennies, Nickels, and Dimes

Name _____

Nickels and Pennies

Under the coins, write the total amount of money so far.
Then write the total using $. The first one is done for you.

6   5¢   5¢   1¢

   <u>5¢</u>   <u>10¢</u>   <u>11¢</u>

$ <u>0</u> . <u>1</u> <u>1</u>
total

---

7   5¢   5¢   1¢   1¢   1¢

_____ _____ _____ _____ _____

$ ___ . ___ ___
total

---

8   5¢   5¢   5¢   1¢   1¢

_____ _____ _____ _____ _____

$ ___ . ___ ___
total

---

9 Maneka has 3 nickels and 6 pennies.

Draw ⑤s and ①s to show her nickels and pennies.

Write the total amount of money.

$ ___ . ___ ___
total

Dimes, Nickels, and Pennies

Under the coins, write the total amount of money so far.
Then write the total using $. The first one is done for you.

10   10¢   5¢   1¢

     10¢   15¢   16¢ $ 0 . 1 6
                                  total

11   10¢   5¢   5¢   1¢   1¢

     _____ _____ _____ _____ _____ $ __ . __ __
                                    total

12   10¢   10¢   10¢   10¢   5¢   1¢

     _____ _____ _____ _____ _____ _____ $ __ . __ __
                                    total

✓ Check Understanding

Draw a collection of 4 dimes, 4 nickels, and 4 pennies.
Show how to count the value of the collection.

PATH to FLUENCY Add Within 100

Add.

1. 36
    + 15

2. 64
    + 23

3. 13
    + 22

4. 47
    + 46

5. 60
    + 18

6. 11
    + 63

7. 28
    + 39

8. 76
    + 23

9. 33
    + 58

10. 63
    + 32

11. 44
    + 27

12. 45
    + 54

PATH to FLUENCY Add Within 100 (continued)

Add.

⑬　49
　+ 51

⑭　58
　+ 26

⑮　12
　+ 85

⑯　28
　+ 31

⑰　65
　+ 16

⑱　42
　+ 26

⑲　77
　+ 19

⑳　27
　+ 53

㉑　35
　+ 40

㉒　33
　+ 67

㉓　24
　+ 19

㉔　82
　+ 7

✔ **Check Understanding**

Make proof drawings to show how adding
26 + 32 is different from adding 26 + 38.

Fluency: Addition Within 100

New Ten Challenge

Work in 👥. Lay out Secret Code Cards like this.

¹⁰ 1 0	⁶⁰ 6 0	¹ 1	⁶ 6
²⁰ 2 0	⁷⁰ 7 0	² 2	⁷ 7
³⁰ 3 0	⁸⁰ 8 0	³ 3	⁸ 8
⁴⁰ 4 0	⁹⁰ 9 0	⁴ 4	⁹ 9
⁵⁰ 5 0		⁵ 5	

1 Use Secret Code Cards to help you make a 2-digit addition (with a sum less than 100).

⁴⁰ 4 0	³ 3
²⁰ 2 0	⁹ 9

$$\begin{array}{r} 43 \\ + 29 \\ \hline 72 \end{array}$$

2 Make another 2-digit addition.

- Use the same tens cards.

- If 👤 *made a new ten,* use ones cards that *do not make a new ten.*

- If 👤 *did not make a new ten,* use ones cards that *make a new ten.*

⁴⁰ 4 0	³ 3
²⁰ 2 0	⁵ 5

$$\begin{array}{r} 43 \\ + 25 \\ \hline 68 \end{array}$$

Activity continues on next page.

New Ten Challenge (continued)

2 Work together to check your work. Correct any errors.

3 Put the Secret Code Cards back. Switch roles and repeat. Continue until time is up.

To play the *New Ten Challenge* as a game and compete with another pair, use the **Scoring Rules** below.

Scoring Rules

for

New Ten Challenge

- Each player: Make two 2-digit additions (following the instructions from Step 1 on p. 125). Do not check your work.

- Trade papers with another pair.

- Put a ✓ next to each correct answer. Put an X next to each incorrect answer.

- Give 1 point for each ✓. Subtract 3 points for each X.

- The pair with more points wins.

Name _____

Practice Adding Three Addends

Add.

1 15 + 29 + 36 = _____

2 24 + 27 + 34 = _____

3 36 + 33 + 39 = _____

4 35 + 26 + 17 = _____

Practice Adding Four Addends

Add.

5 $18 + 23 + 34 + 17 =$ _____

6 $38 + 32 + 14 + 25 =$ _____

7 $20 + 16 + 33 + 27 =$ _____

8 $26 + 41 + 35 + 12 =$ _____

✔ **Check Understanding**

Make two different proof drawings to show two different ways to find the sum of $17 + 49 + 23$.

Add Three or Four 2-Digit Addends

Name _____

Solve Problems and Compare Methods

To recycle means to use again. The second graders at Center School are collecting trash. They will recycle the trash to make musical instruments.

Collected So Far
102 water bottles
88 pie plates
63 paper towel rolls

Water Bottle
Maracas

Paper Towel
Roll Kazoo

Pie Plate
Tambourine

Solve each word problem.

1. There are 48 children that each want to make a tambourine. Each tambourine is made with 2 pie plates. Do they have enough pie plates?

   Circle yes or no.　　　　yes　no

2. If the children collect 10 more water bottles, how many water bottles will they have?

   ☐ _____
   　　label

3. If the children collect 29 more paper towel rolls, will they have enough to make 75 kazoos?

   Circle yes or no.　　　　yes　no

Money for Cans and Bottles

Some states help people recycle by giving money back when they return a bottle or can. This fleece jacket, this yo-yo, and this park bench are all made from recycled plastic bottles.

Solve each word problem.

4 Suzanne and Jing get 5 cents for each can or bottle they return. Suzanne returns 29 cans and 18 bottles. Jing returns 15 cans and 34 bottles. Who gets more money back?

_____

5 Malia returns 12 bottles. She gets one nickel for each bottle. How much money does she get?

_____

6 Roberto gets 5 cents for every can he returns. He gets $1.20. How many cans does he return?

☐ _____
      label

Focus on Mathematical Practices

Name _____

Date _____

Add.

1.   48
   + 26
   -----

2. 23 + 18 + 64 = _____

_____

Solve each word problem.   **Show your work.**

3. Molly has 1 dollar, 1 dime, and 5 pennies.
   How much money does Molly have?
   Use $ in your answer.

   _____

_____

4. Leah has 2 dimes, 3 nickels, and 1 penny.
   How much money does Leah have?
   Use ¢ in your answer.

   _____

_____

5. The cost of one ball is a dime. Rob buys 5 balls.
   How much money does Rob spend?
   Use ¢ in your answer.

   _____

Name _____ **Date** _____

PATH to
FLUENCY

Add or subtract.

1 $9 + 8 =$ ☐   **2** $7 + 5 =$ ☐   **3** $8 + 8 =$ ☐

4 $11 - 4 =$ ☐   **5** $20 - 7 =$ ☐   **6** $12 - 6 =$ ☐

7
$$\begin{array}{r} 16 \\ -2 \\ \hline \end{array}$$

8
$$\begin{array}{r} 15 \\ -12 \\ \hline \end{array}$$

9
$$\begin{array}{r} 17 \\ -7 \\ \hline \end{array}$$

10
$$\begin{array}{r} 33 \\ +11 \\ \hline \end{array}$$

11
$$\begin{array}{r} 57 \\ +12 \\ \hline \end{array}$$

12
$$\begin{array}{r} 37 \\ +21 \\ \hline \end{array}$$

13
$$\begin{array}{r} 37 \\ +48 \\ \hline \end{array}$$

14
$$\begin{array}{r} 18 \\ +16 \\ \hline \end{array}$$

15
$$\begin{array}{r} 28 \\ +69 \\ \hline \end{array}$$

1 Choose the ways that show 147.

○ one hundred seventy-four

○ 100 + 40 + 7

○

○ one hundred forty-seven

○ 100 + 70 + 4

---

2 Draw 124 using Quick Hundreds, Quick Tens, and circles. Write the number name. Then write the number in expanded form.

Write a symbol from a tile to compare numbers.

3 131 $\bigcirc$ 124   **4** 187 $\bigcirc$ 187

5 118 $\bigcirc$ 128   **6** 186 $\bigcirc$ 168

7 Match each addition problem to its total on the right.

$$\begin{array}{r} 63 \\ + 25 \\ \hline \end{array}$$ •   • 182

$$\begin{array}{r} 48 \\ + 36 \\ \hline \end{array}$$ •   • 88

$94 + 11$ •   • 84

$85 + 97$ •   • 105

8 Explain how to add $28 + 97$.
Then make a proof drawing.

Circle the correct sum.

⑨ 22 + 64 + 37 = | 87
| 113
| 123

⑩ 35 + 43 + 22 + 11 = | 101
| 111
| 113

Skip count by 5s.

⑪ 25 _____ _____ _____ _____ _____ 55

Solve.

⑫ Sara has these coins. She has exactly enough to buy a pencil.
Under the coins, write the total amount of money so far.

10¢   5¢   5¢   1¢   1¢

_____ _____ _____ _____ _____

What is the price of the pencil?
Use ¢ in your answer.

---

⑬ Scott has 44¢. List 3 different combinations
of coins that Scott could have.

[ ] dimes   [ ] nickels   [ ] pennies

[ ] dimes   [ ] nickels   [ ] pennies

[ ] dimes   [ ] nickels   [ ] pennies

⑭ Chris buys a folder that costs $1.23.
She has these coins and bills. Circle the
coins and bills Chris can use to buy the folder.

Write how much money Chris has left using $. $ ___ . ___ ___

⑮ Chen makes 38 red paper birds.
He makes 25 yellow paper birds.
How many paper birds does he make in all?
Show two methods you can use to find the answer.

```
┌──────────────────────────────────────────┐
│                                          │
│                                          │
│                                          │
│                                          │
│   ┌────┐                                 │
│   │    │  _____               │
│   └────┘     label                       │
└──────────────────────────────────────────┘
```

Adding Apples

Write a 2-digit number in each ☐.

Use any method to solve each word problem.

Show your work.

1 Martin picks ☐ apples.

Mindy picks ☐ apples.

How many apples do they pick in all?

☐ _____
  label

Explain your method.

_____

_____

2 Kelly puts ☐ apples in a box.

Allie puts ☐ apples in the same box.

Cory puts in ☐ apples.

How many apples do they put in the box altogether?

☐ _____
  label

Explain your method.

_____

_____

3 Write an addition word problem about apples.
Use 2-digit numbers in your problem.
Then solve.

_____

_____

_____

_____

4 Make a proof drawing to show how you solved your
word problem.

Dear Family:

Your child is working on a geometry and measurement unit. In this unit, children will use rulers to measure line segments and draw shapes. They will learn about both centimeters and inches.

In Lesson 1, children will work with centimeter units. Through practice, they will learn that when they use a centimeter ruler to measure line segments, they are counting the number of 1-cm length units that comprise the segment.

A ruler shows repeated units of length.

As children measure, compare, and add the lengths of objects, they begin to develop an understanding of the importance of measurement. You can help your child link the measurement and geometry concepts learned in school with the real world. Discuss the lengths of different objects in your home. Talk about objects that are longer or shorter than other objects. Also encourage your child to find examples of different shapes (triangles, quadrilaterals including rectangles and squares, pentagons, and hexagons) in your home or neighborhood. This will help your child enjoy and understand geometry.

If you have any questions or comments, please contact me. Thank you.

Sincerely,
Your child's teacher

CC SS Unit 3 addresses the following standards from the Common Core State Standards for Mathematics: **2.OA.B.2, 2.NBT.B.5, 2.NBT.B.7, 2.MD.A.1, 2.MD.A.2, 2.MD.A.3, 2.MD.A.4, 2.MD.D.9, 2.G.A.1,** and all Mathematical Practices.

Estimada familia:

Su niño está trabajando en una unidad que trata sobre geometría y medidas. En esta unidad los niños usarán reglas en centímetros para medir segmentos y trazar figuras. Aprenderán acerca de los centímetros y de las pulgadas.

En la Lección 1, los niños trabajarán con unidades de centímetros. A través de la práctica, aprenderán que cuando usan una regla en centímetros para medir segmentos, están contando el número de unidades de la longitud de 1 cm que componen el segmento.

Una regla muestra las unidades repetidas de longitud.

A medida que los niños miden, comparan y agregan las longitudes de los objetos, comienzan a desarrollar la comprensión de la importancia de la medición. Usted puede ayudar a su niño a relacionar los conceptos de medición y geometría aprendidos en la escuela con el mundo real. Comenten sobre las longitudes de los diferentes objetos en su casa. Hablen sobre los objetos que son más largos o más cortos que otros objetos. También anime a su niño a buscar ejemplos de diferentes figuras (triángulos, cuadriláteros incluyendo rectángulos y cuadrados, pentágonos y hexágonos) en su casa o en el vecindario. Esto ayudará a su niño a disfrutar y comprender la geometría.

Si tiene alguna pregunta o algún comentario, por favor comuníquese conmigo. Gracias.

Atentamente,
El maestro de su niño

CC SS En la Unidad 3 se aplican los siguientes estándares de los Estándares estatales comunes de matemáticas: **2.OA.B.2, 2.NBT.B.5, 2.NBT.B.7, 2.MD.A.1, 2.MD.A.2, 2.MD.A.3, 2.MD.A.4, 2.MD.D.9, 2.G.A.1** y todos los de Prácticas matemáticas.

angle	hexagon
centimeter (cm)	inch (in.)
foot (ft)	length

A hexagon has 6 sides and 6 angles.

These are angles.

1 inch

1 cm

The length of the pencil is about 17 cm. (not to scale)

foot

12 inches = 1 foot (not drawn to scale)

line plot

pentagon

line segment

quadrilateral

opposite
sides

rectangle

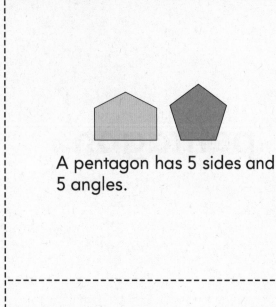

A pentagon has 5 sides and 5 angles.

Length of Shoelaces (inches)

A quadrilateral has 4 sides and 4 angles.

A rectangle has 4 sides and 4 right angles. Opposite sides have the same length.

opposite sides

© Houghton Mifflin Harcourt Publishing Company

rectangular prism	triangle
right angle	view
square	yard (yd)

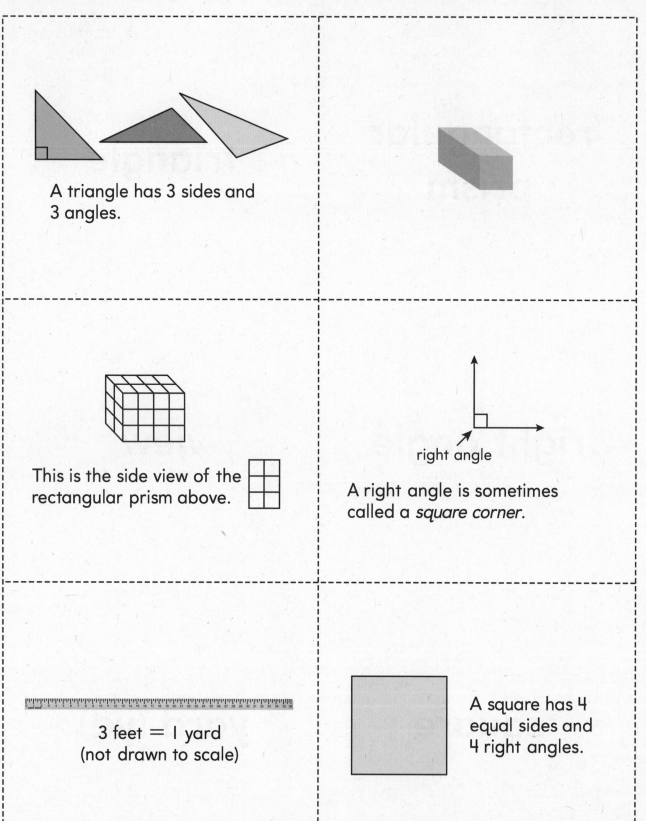

A triangle has 3 sides and 3 angles.

This is the side view of the rectangular prism above.

right angle

A right angle is sometimes called a *square corner*.

3 feet = 1 yard
(not drawn to scale)

A square has 4 equal sides and 4 right angles.

Name _____

Measure and Find Difference in Length

A **centimeter** is a unit of measure for **length**.
The short way to write centimeters is **cm**.

I cm

To find the measure of the **line segment**,
count the 1-cm lengths.

A ruler shows 1-cm lengths.
The 1-cm lengths are marked.

0   1   2   3   4   5   6   7   8

Count the 1-cm lengths. Write the length.

1   ☐ cm

2   ☐ cm

Use a centimeter ruler to mark the 1-cm lengths. Write the length.

3   ☐ cm

4   ☐ cm

Use a Ruler to Find Difference in Length

You can use a ruler to draw a line segment 7 cm long.
Begin drawing at the zero edge of your ruler.
Stop when you have counted seven 1-cm lengths.

Use your centimeter ruler to draw a line segment
with the length given. Mark the 1-cm lengths.

5 8 cm

6 5 cm

7 How many centimeters longer is the line segment
in Exercise 5 than in Exercise 6? ☐ cm

Draw a line segment with the length given.

8 6 cm

9 2 cm

10 How many centimeters longer is the line segment
in Exercise 8 than in Exercise 9? ☐ cm

© Houghton Mifflin Harcourt Publishing Company

Measure Length

Name _____

Measure Objects and Find Difference in Length

Measure the object. Write the length.
Circle the shorter object.

⑪

_____ cm

_____ cm

⑫ The _____ pencil is ☐ cm shorter.

Measure the object. Write the length.
Circle the longer object.

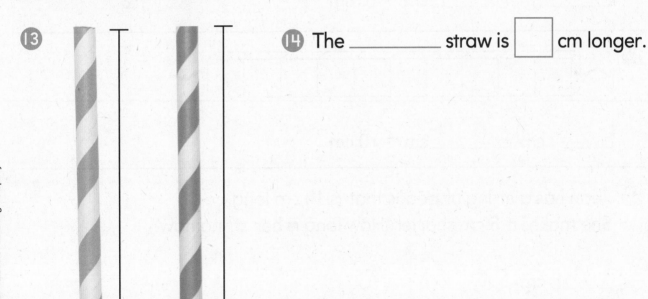

⑬

⑭ The _____ straw is ☐ cm longer.

_____ cm

_____ cm

Partners and Adding Lengths

Lee wants to make a string of beads 10 cm long. He has red and blue beads that are each 1 cm long. Color the beads to show 3 different ways he can make the string. Complete the equation to show how he made the string with the two colors.

15

_____ cm + _____ cm = 10 cm

16

_____ cm + _____ cm = 10 cm

17

_____ cm + _____ cm = 10 cm

18 Jean has a string of beads that is 14 cm long. She makes it 8 cm shorter. How long is her string now?

_____ cm

✓ Check Understanding

Explain how to find how much longer a 10-cm length is than a 3-cm length.

Measure Length

Name _____

VOCABULARY
square
right angle
angle

Draw and Identify Squares

A **square** is a shape with 4 equal sides and
4 **right angles**.

1. Use your centimeter ruler. Draw a square with sides
that are each 3 cm long.

Look at these shapes.

2. Are any of these shapes squares? _____

3. How are the **angles** of these shapes different

   from the angles of squares? _____

   _____

4. How are the sides of these shapes different from the

   sides of squares? _____

   _____

5. Is this shape a square? Explain why or why not.

   _____

   _____

Draw and Identify Rectangles

VOCABULARY
rectangle
opposite sides

A **rectangle** is a shape with 4 sides and 4 right angles. It has **opposite sides** that are equal in length.

6 Use your centimeter ruler to draw a rectangle that is 6 cm long and 3 cm wide.

Look at these shapes.

7 Are these shapes rectangles? Explain why or why not.

_____

_____

8 Is a square a rectangle? Explain why or why not.

_____

_____

_____

Recognize and Draw Shapes

Name _____

Compare Lengths of Sides of Triangles

VOCABULARY
triangle

A **triangle** is a shape with 3 angles and 3 sides.
All of these shapes are triangles.

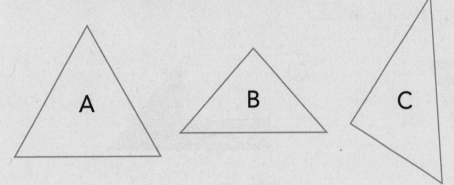

9 Measure each side of Triangle A.
What did you discover about the sides?

_____

_____

10 Measure each side of Triangle B.
What did you discover about the sides?

_____

_____

11 Measure each side of Triangle C.
What did you discover about the sides?

_____

_____

12 Draw a loop to show how much longer the longest side
of Triangle C is than the shortest side. The longest side

of Triangle C is ☐ cm longer than its shortest side.

Describe Shapes

VOCABULARY
quadrilateral
pentagon
hexagon

A **quadrilateral** is a shape with 4 sides.
A **pentagon** is a shape with 5 sides.
A **hexagon** is a shape with 6 sides.

How many sides? _____
How many angles? _____
Loop the shape.
   quadrilateral
   square
   hexagon

How many sides? _____
How many angles? _____
Loop the shape.
   quadrilateral
   pentagon
   triangle

How many sides? _____
How many angles? _____
Loop the shape.
   hexagon
   triangle
   rectangle

How many sides? _____
How many angles? _____
Loop the shape.
   rectangle
   pentagon
   quadrilateral

 Check Understanding

Draw a pentagon and a hexagon. How are the shapes alike? How are they different?

Recognize and Draw Shapes

Estimate and Measure Around a Square

Find the distance around each square.

1

A

___ cm

___ cm

B

D

___ cm

___ cm

C

___ cm + ___ cm + ___ cm + ___ cm

= ___ cm

2

I ___ cm J

___ cm

___ cm

L ___ cm K

___ cm + ___ cm + ___ cm + ___ cm

= ___ cm

Estimate and then measure each side.
Then find the distance around the square.

3 **a.** Complete the table. Use a
centimeter ruler to measure.

Side	Estimate	Measure
EF		
FG		
GH		
HE		

E ___ cm F

___ cm ___ cm

H ___ cm G

b. Find the distance around the square.

___ cm + ___ cm + ___ cm + ___ cm = ___ cm

Content Standards **2.OA.B.2, 2.MD.A.1, 2.MD.A.3**
Mathematical Practices **MP1, MP2, MP3, MP6, MP7**

Estimate and Measure Around a Rectangle

Find the distance around each rectangle.

4

___ cm + ___ cm + ___ cm + ___ cm

= ___ cm

5

___ cm + ___ cm + ___ cm + ___ cm

= ___ cm

Estimate and then measure each side.

Then find the distance around the rectangle.

6 a. Complete the table. Use a centimeter ruler to measure.

Side	Estimate	Measure
WX		
XY		
YZ		
ZW		

b. Find the distance around the rectangle.

___ cm + ___ cm + ___ cm + ___ cm = ___ cm

Check Understanding

Explain how to estimate the length in centimeters of a side of a square.

Estimate and Measure

Estimate and Measure

Find the distance around each triangle.

1

2

_____ cm + _____ cm + _____ cm

= _____ cm

_____ cm + _____ cm + _____ cm

= _____ cm

Estimate and then measure each side.

Then find the distance around the triangle.

3 a. Complete the table.

Side	Estimate	Measure
HI		
IJ		
JH		

b. Find the distance around the triangle.

_____ cm + _____ cm + _____ cm = _____ cm

Estimate and Measure (continued)

4 **a.** Complete the table.

Side	Estimate	Measure
LM		
MO		
OL		

b. Find the distance around the triangle.

_____ cm + _____ cm + _____ cm = _____ cm

5 **a.** Complete the table.

Side	Estimate	Measure
PQ		
QR		
RP		

b. Find the distance around the triangle.

_____ cm + _____ cm + _____ cm = _____ cm

✓ **Check Understanding**

Draw two different triangles. Each triangle must have one side 3 cm long and another side 4 cm long.

Draw, Estimate, and Measure

Name _____

Rectangular Prisms

Cut on solid lines.
Fold on dashed lines.

CC SS Content Standards **2.G.A.1**
Mathematical Practices **MP3, MP5, MP6**

Rectangular Prisms **153**

Rectangular Prisms

Name _____

Build and Draw Rectangular Prisms

VOCABULARY
rectangular prism
view

Using unit cubes, build a **rectangular prism** to match each description. Draw the rectangular prism from the top **view**, front view, and side view.

1 two rows of three unit cubes

| top view | front view | side view |

2 one row of two unit cubes stacked on top of another row of two unit cubes

| top view | front view | side view |

Build Rectangular Prisms from Drawings

Build a rectangular prism to match each set of views.

3 **top view**   **front view**   **side view**

4 **top view**   **front view**   **side view**

Draw Using Faces **155**

Identify Shapes

A	B	C
D	E	F
G	H	I
J	K	L

✔ Check Understanding

Shape C has _____ sides and _____ angles.

It is a _____.

Draw Using Faces

1 Measure each string to the nearest centimeter.

[ ] cm

[ ] cm

2 Look at Exercise 1. How much longer is the first string than the second string?

[ ] cm

3 Name the shape. Choose a word from the box.

cube	hexagon	triangle
pentagon	quadrilateral	

_____

4 What is the distance around the triangle?

2 cm + [ ] cm + [ ] cm = [ ] cm

5 What shape has this set of views?

top view   front view   side view

[ ] [ ] [ ]

_____

Name _____ Date _____

Add or subtract.

1 $3 + 3 = \boxed{}$ **2** $9 + 7 = \boxed{}$ **3** $7 + 5 = \boxed{}$

4 $11 - 7 = \boxed{}$ **5** $10 - 7 = \boxed{}$ **6** $18 - 9 = \boxed{}$

7
$$\begin{array}{r} 19 \\ -13 \\ \hline \end{array}$$

8
$$\begin{array}{r} 18 \\ -16 \\ \hline \end{array}$$

9
$$\begin{array}{r} 20 \\ -7 \\ \hline \end{array}$$

10
$$\begin{array}{r} 30 \\ +10 \\ \hline \end{array}$$

11
$$\begin{array}{r} 65 \\ +17 \\ \hline \end{array}$$

12
$$\begin{array}{r} 33 \\ +15 \\ \hline \end{array}$$

13
$$\begin{array}{r} 67 \\ +32 \\ \hline \end{array}$$

14
$$\begin{array}{r} 18 \\ +16 \\ \hline \end{array}$$

15
$$\begin{array}{r} 58 \\ +38 \\ \hline \end{array}$$

Dear Family:

In this unit, your child will be collecting measurement data and using that data to make line plots. A *line plot* is a display that uses a number line and dots (or other marks) to represent data. For this reason, line plots are sometimes called *dot plots*.

Your child will be asked to bring one or two pencils to school. The length of each pencil should be more than 1 inch and less than 8 inches. Children will work in small groups. They will measure each pencil brought in by the members of their group and then make a line plot similar to the one shown below.

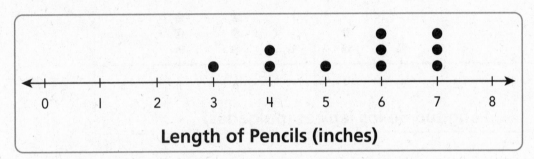

Length of Pencils (inches)

In this unit, your child will also be given several experiences that will help build understanding that the smaller the unit used to measure a given length or distance, the more of those units will be needed.

So, for example, since centimeters are shorter than inches, when the paintbrush below is measured in both centimeters and inches, the number of centimeters is more than the number of inches.

Sincerely,
Your child's teacher

CC SS Unit 3 addresses the following standards from the Common Core State Standards for Mathematics: **2.OA.B.2, 2.NBT.B.5, 2.NBT.B.7, 2.MD.A.1, 2.MD.A.2, 2.MD.A.3, 2.MD.A.4, 2.MD.D.9, 2.G.A.1, and all** Mathematical Practices.

Estimate and Measure with Centimeters **159**

Estimada familia:

En esta unidad, su niño reunirá datos sobre medidas y usará esos datos para hacer diagramas de puntos. Un *diagrama de puntos* es un diagrama que usa una recta numérica y puntos u otras marcas para representar datos.

Se le pedirá a su niño que traiga uno o dos lápices a la escuela. Cada lápiz debe medir más de 1 pulgada de longitud pero menos de 8. Los niños trabajarán en grupos pequeños. Medirán los lápices de cada miembro de su grupo y luego, harán un diagrama de puntos como el que se muestra debajo.

Longitud de los lápices (pulgadas)

También en esta unidad, a su niño se le brindarán diversas experiencias que lo ayudarán a comprender que entre más pequeña sea la unidad que se use para medir una determinada longitud o distancia, más de esas unidades se necesitarán.

Entonces, por ejemplo, como los centímetros son más cortos que las pulgadas, cuando el pincel de abajo se mide en centímetros y en pulgadas, el número de centímetros es mayor que el número de pulgadas.

Atentamente,
El maestro de su niño

En la Unidad 3 se aplican los siguientes estándares de los Estándares estatales comunes de matemáticas: **2.OA.B.2, 2.NBT.B.5, 2.NBT.B.7, 2.MD.A.1, 2.MD.A.2, 2.MD.A.3, 2.MD.A.4, 2.MD.D.9, 2.G.A.1 y todos los de** Prácticas matemáticas.

Estimate and Measure with Centimeters

Column 1 (left markers): 25↑ 24 23 22 21 20 19 18 17 16 15 14 13 12 11 10 9 8 7 6 5 4 3 2 1

50 (rotated)
20 (rotated)
10 (rotated)

50↑ 49 48 47 46 45 44 43 42 41 40 39 38 37 36 35 34 33 32 31 30 29 28 27 26 25↓

30 (rotated)
40 (rotated)

75↑ 74 73 72 71 70 69 68 67 66 65 64 63 62 61 60 59 58 57 56 55 54 53 52 51 50↓

70 (rotated)
60 (rotated)

100↑ 99 98 97 96 95 94 93 92 91 90 89 88 87 86 85 84 83 82 81 80 79 78 77 76 75↓

100 (rotated)
90 (rotated)
80 (rotated)

Step 1: Cut out on the dashed lines.

Step 2: Put the sections in order.

Step 3: Tape or paste the sections together.

← 100
← 76
← 74   Tape or paste
← 51
← 49   Tape or paste
← 26
← 24   Tape or paste
← 1

Meter Tape (Vertical)

Meter Tape (Vertical)

Name _____

Estimate and Measure

Find a part of your hand that is about each length.

1 1 cm _____

2 10 cm _____

Find a part of your body that is about 1 meter long.

3 1 m _____

Find the real object. Circle the name of the tool you will use to measure in centimeters. Measure the object.

4

meter stick
centimeter ruler

_____ cm

5

meter stick
centimeter ruler

_____ cm

6

meter stick
centimeter ruler

_____ cm

7

meter stick
centimeter ruler

_____ m

8 Find an object longer than 10 cm and shorter than 30 cm. Draw the object.

Measure Heights

Use the meter sticks at the stations to measure heights.

9 Complete the table for each person in your group.

Person's Name	Estimated Height (cm)	Actual Height (cm)

Use the table to answer these questions.

10 What is the height of the tallest person in your group?

_____

11 How much taller is the tallest person than the shortest person? Find the difference by subtracting.

_____

What's the Error?

12 Puzzled Penguin measures the height of this bookcase and says it is 38 cm tall. What was Puzzled Penguin's mistake?

Did I make a mistake?

_____

_____

_____

Estimate and Measure with Centimeters

Name _____

Introduce Line Plots

VOCABULARY
line plot

Look at this **line plot**.

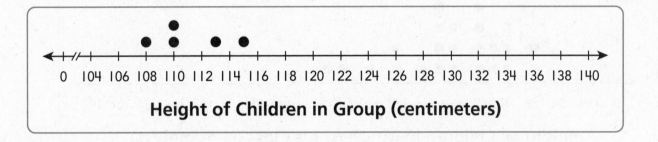

Height of Children in Group (centimeters)

Make a Line Plot

13 Draw dots for the heights of the children in your group. Use data from the table on page 164.

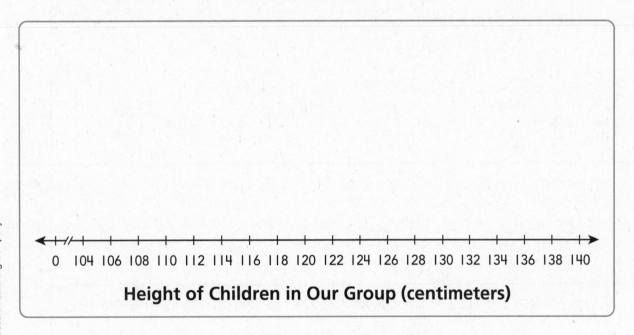

Height of Children in Our Group (centimeters)

14 Which height in your group is the greatest? _____ cm

15 Which height in your group is the least? _____ cm

Estimate and Measure with Centimeters **165**

Discuss a Line Plot

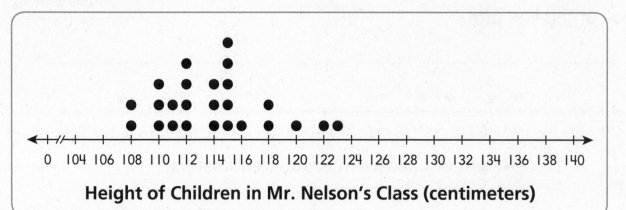

Height of Children in Mr. Nelson's Class (centimeters)

Show Class Data on a Line Plot

16 Draw dots for the heights of the children in your class.

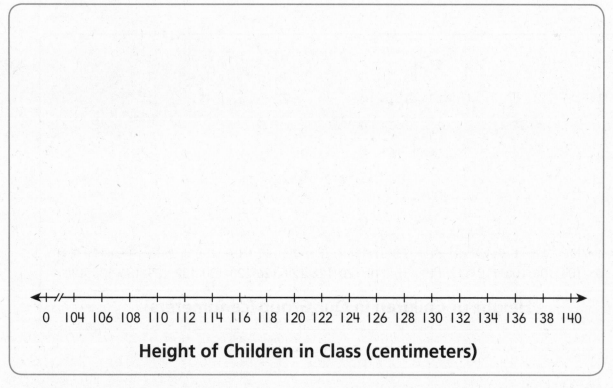

Height of Children in Class (centimeters)

 Check Understanding

Write a question about the class line plot. Trade questions with a partner, and answer your partner's question.

Estimate and Measure with Centimeters

Name _____

Make an Inch Ruler

Directions:

Step 1: Cut along the dashed lines.

Step 2: Place the sections in the correct order.

Step 3: Tape or glue together the sections at the tab.

Step 4: Write a **6** where the two strips meet.

TAB

5

4

3

2

1

0

12

11

10

9

8

7

TAB

5

4

3

2

1

0

12

11

10

9

8

7

Content Standards 2.MD.A.1, 2.MD.A.2, 2.MD.A.3, 2.MD.D.9
Mathematical Practices MP2, MP3, MP5, MP6, MP7, MP8

Inch Ruler

Measure to the Nearest Inch

VOCABULARY
inch (in.)

To measure to the nearest **inch (in.)**, place the zero mark on your ruler at the left end of the object. Find the inch mark that is closest to the right end of the object.

To the nearest inch, the length of this toy car is 2 inches.
Measure the length of each object below to the nearest inch.

1. _____

2. _____

3. _____

4 Draw a horizontal line segment that is 2 in. long.

5 Draw a horizontal line segment that is 6 in. long.

Estimate and Measure in Inches

6 Describe a part of your hand that measures about 2 in.

_____

7 Describe a part of your hand that measures about 1 in.

_____

8 Describe a part of your hand that measures about 6 in.

_____

Estimate and measure the length of each line segment.

9 ├───────────────────┤

Estimated length: _____   Measured length: _____

10 ├─────────────────────────┤

Estimated length: _____   Measured length: _____

11 Find four classroom objects that you can measure in inches and then in centimeters. Choose two objects with a length between 12 inches and 24 inches. Complete the table.

Object	Estimated length (in.)	Measured length (in.)	Measured length (cm)

Estimate and Measure with Inches

Name _____

Make a Yardstick

Directions:

Step 1: Cut along the dashed lines.

Step 2: Place the sections in the correct order.

Step 3: Tape or glue together the sections at the tab.

TAB	TAB	TAB	TAB	TAB	
	1 ft		2 ft		36 3 ft
5	11	17	23	29	35
4	10	16	22	28	34
3	9	15	21	27	33
2	8	14	20	26	32
1	7	13	19	25	31
	6		18		30
0					

Yardstick

Name _____

Measure in Feet and Yards

Find each length to the nearest **foot (ft)**.

VOCABULARY
foot (ft)
yard (yd)

12 width of your desk

13 length from your knee to your ankle

_____

Find each length to the nearest **yard (yd)**.

14 height of the classroom door

15 length of a bookshelf

_____

Measure each length to the nearest foot and to the nearest yard.

16 width of the classroom door

17 length of the classroom board

_____ ft

_____ ft

_____ yd

_____ yd

18 What do you notice about the numbers when you measure in yards instead of feet? Why?

_____

_____

Estimate and Measure Height

Estimate your height in inches. Then work with a partner to find your actual height.

19 Estimate: _____

20 Actual height: _____

Height in Centimeters and Inches

Draw a dot to show your height in centimeters.

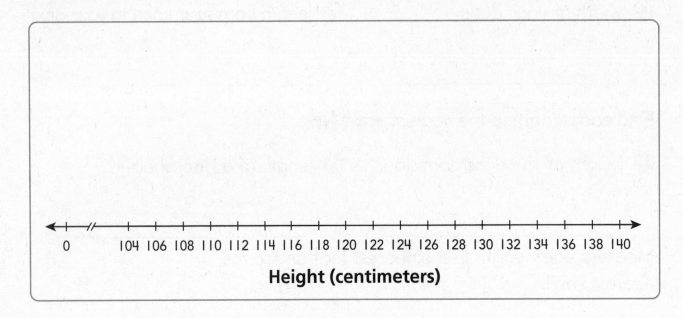

Height (centimeters)

Draw a dot to show your height in inches.

Height (inches)

 Check Understanding

Is a 20-inch piece of string *more* or *less*
than 20 cm long? Explain how you know.

Estimate and Measure with Inches

Name _____

Lengths of Pencils

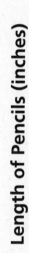

0   1   2   3   4   5   6   7   8

Length of Pencils (inches)

0 1 2 3 4 5 6 7 8 9 10 11 12 13 14 15 16 17 18 19 20

Length of Pencils (centimeters)

CC SS Content Standards **2.MD.A.1, 2.MD.A.2, 2.MD.A.3, 2.MD.D.9**
Mathematical Practices **MP2, MP4, MP5, MP7, MP8**

Widths of Books

Width of Books (inches)

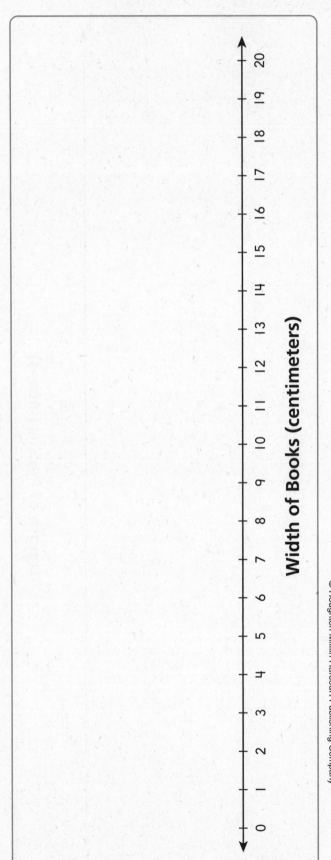

Width of Books (centimeters)

Measure for and Make Line Plots

Name _____

Measurement Data on Line Plots

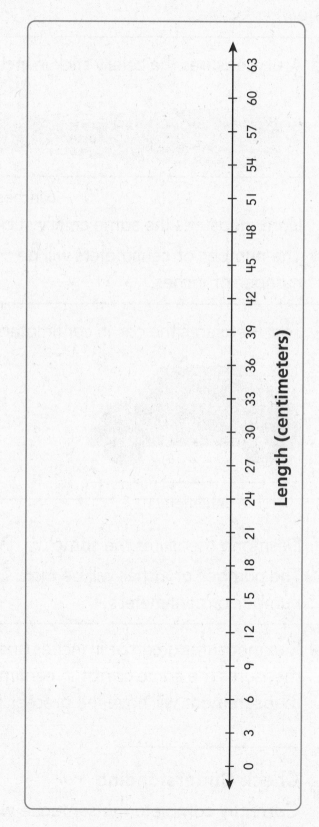

Measure for and Make Line Plots **177**

Compare Measurement Units

Ring *more* or *less*.

---

1 Arul measures the celery stick in inches.

6 inches

Liam measures the same celery stick in centimeters.

The number of centimeters will be *more less* than the number of inches.

---

2 Jael measures the car in centimeters.

6 centimeters

Desmond measures the same car in inches.
The number of inches will be *more less* than the number of centimeters.

---

3 Rue measures a carrot in inches and Peter measures the same carrot in centimeters. Whose measurement will have the greater number of units?

_____

✔ **Check Understanding**

Correctly complete the sentence with *more* or *less*.

9 feet is _____ than 9 yards.

Name _____

Identify Quilt Shapes

A patchwork quilt is made by sewing pieces of cloth together. Look for shapes in these patchwork quilts.

1 Color each shape a different color.

Shape	triangle	quadrilateral	pentagon	hexagon
Color	red	orange	blue	yellow

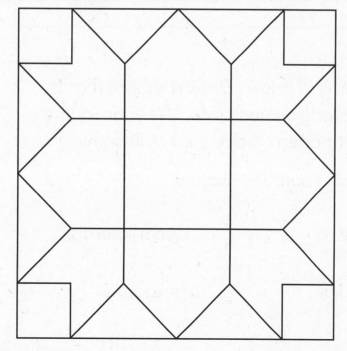

© Houghton Mifflin Harcourt Publishing Company

Make Quilts

2 Continue the pattern to complete this quilt square.

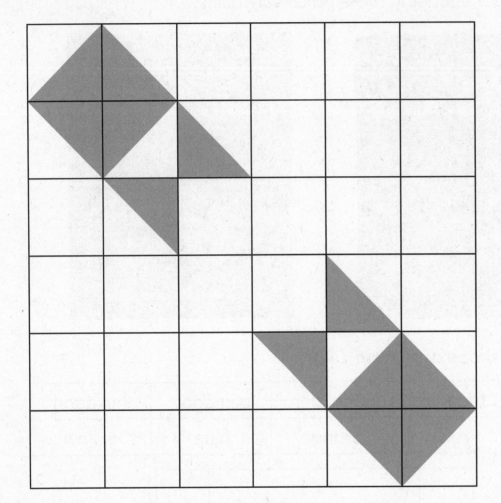

3 Use centimeter grid paper. Draw a square that is 16 centimeters long on each side. Use your square to make a quilt pattern. Color your quilt square.

When you finish, count the shapes.

_____ triangles   _____ quadrilaterals

_____ pentagons   _____ hexagons

Focus on Mathematical Practices

Name _____ Date _____

Solve.

① Estimate and then measure the length of the marker.

Estimate: ☐ inches

Measure: ☐ inches

② Estimate and then measure the length of the chalk.

Estimate: ☐ centimeters

Measure: ☐ centimeters

③ Estimate the width of a desk in feet.

Estimate: ☐ feet

④ Describe a classroom object that measures about 2 meters.

_____

⑤ Describe a classroom object that measures about 2 feet.

_____

Name _____   Date _____

Add or subtract.

1 4 + 1 = ☐

2 11 + 9 = ☐

3 9 + 7 = ☐

4 12 − 4 = ☐

5 10 − 8 = ☐

6 17 − 10 = ☐

7
```
   14
 −  9
```

8
```
   18
 − 14
```

9
```
   20
 −  8
```

10
```
   40
 + 20
```

11
```
   48
 + 27
```

12
```
   27
 + 32
```

13
```
   69
 + 24
```

14
```
   18
 +  2
```

15
```
   54
 + 46
```

Measure each string to the nearest centimeter.
Then match the string to its length on the right.

1   •   • 6 cm

2   •   • 2 cm

3   •   • 3 cm

4   •   • 5 cm

5   •   • 4 cm

---

6 Show the lengths of the five strings on this line plot.

Length of Strings (centimeters)

How many strings are longer than 3 cm?

☐ strings

7 Estimate the length of the eraser in inches.

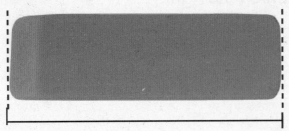

Write your estimate.

about ⬜ _____
       label

Measure the eraser to the nearest inch.
Circle the actual measure.

The eraser is | 3
               4 | inches long.
               5

---

8 Measure each pencil in inches.

⬜ inches

⬜ inches

Is the sentence true? Choose Yes or No.

The yellow pencil is 2 inches longer than the blue pencil.	○ Yes	○ No
The yellow pencil is 1 inch longer than the blue pencil.	○ Yes	○ No
The blue pencil is 2 inches shorter than the yellow pencil.	○ Yes	○ No

9 Draw each shape in the correct box below.

Has exactly 6 sides	Has exactly 4 angles	Has fewer than 4 angles

10 Measure the crayon in centimeters and in inches.

Circle the number or words in each box that makes the sentence true.

The crayon is
| 8 |
| 9 |
| 10 |
centimeters long.

The crayon is
| 3 |
| 4 |
| 5 |
inches long.

There are fewer
| inches than centimeters |
| centimeters than inches |
because
| inches are bigger than centimeters. |
| centimeters are bigger than inches. |

Name the shapes using the words on the tiles.

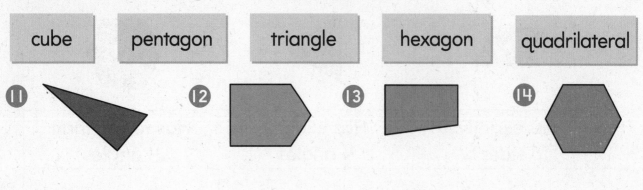

| cube | pentagon | triangle | hexagon | quadrilateral |

11. _____

12. _____

13. _____

14. _____

15. Complete the table. Use an inch ruler to measure.

Side	Estimate	Measure
EF		
FG		
GH		
HE		

E _____ in. F

_____ in.   _____ in.

H   G

_____ in.

Find the distance around the square. Show your work.

The distance around the square is [   ] inches.

Name _____

Setting Up the Table

8 people can sit at this table.	10 people can sit at this table.

1. Draw a rectangular table that seats 12 people with no extra places.

. . . .

. . . .

. . . .

. . . .

2. Can the table be a square and seat exactly 12 people? Explain your answer.

_____

_____

_____

3. Find the distance around the rectangular table you drew in centimeters and in inches.

_____ cm   about _____ in.

Explain why the number of centimeters is different from the number of inches.

_____

_____

Caitlin is sitting at a table shaped like a quadrilateral.
She uses an inch ruler to draw a model of the table.

4 Measure the length of each side.
Then find the distance around the table in
Caitlin's drawing.

[ ] in. + [ ] in. + [ ] in. + [ ] in. = [ ] in.

5 Mr. Evans puts two tables together to form a bigger table.

What shape is the table now? _____

6 Draw another table connected to the table Caitlin drew.
You can arrange them like Mr. Evans did, or choose an
arrangement of your own.

What is the distance around your new bigger table?
Show your work.

_____ inches

© Houghton Mifflin Harcourt Publishing Company

Addition and Subtraction Problem Types

	Result Unknown	Change Unknown	Start Unknown
Add To	Aisha has 46 stamps in her collection. Then her grandfather gives her 29 stamps. How many stamps does she have now? *Situation and Solution Equation:* $46 + 29 = \square$	Aisha has 46 stamps in her collection. Then her grandfather gives her some stamps. Now she has 75 stamps. How many stamps did her grandfather give her? *Situation Equation:* $46 + \square = 75$ *Solution Equation:* $\square = 75 - 46$	Aisha has some stamps in her collection. Then her grandfather gives her 29 stamps. Now she has 75 stamps. How many stamps did she have to start? *Situation Equation:* $\square + 29 = 75$ *Solution Equation:* $\square = 75 - 29$
Take From	A store has 43 bottles of water at the start of the day. During the day, the store sells 25 bottles. How many bottles do they have at the end of the day? *Situation and Solution Equation:* $43 - 25 = \square$	A store has 43 bottles of water at the start of the day. The store has 18 bottles left at the end of the day. How many bottles does the store sell? *Situation Equation:* $43 - \square = 18$ *Solution Equation:* $\square = 43 - 18$	A store sells 25 bottles of water during one day. At the end of the day 18 bottles are left. How many bottles did the store have at the beginning of the day? *Situation Equation:* $\square - 25 = 18$ *Solution Equation:* $\square = 25 + 18$

[1]A situation equation represents the structure (action) in the problem situation. A solution equation shows the operation used to find the answer.

Addition and Subtraction Problem Types (continued)

	Total Unknown	Addend Unknown	Other Addend Unknown
| **Put Together/ Take Apart** | A clothing store has 39 shirts with short sleeves and 45 shirts with long sleeves. How many shirts does the store have in all?<br><br>*Math Drawing²:*<br><br>```
     □
    / \
   /   \
  39    45
```<br><br>*Situation and Solution Equation:*<br>$39 + 45 = \square$ | Of the 84 shirts in a clothing store, 39 have short sleeves. The rest have long sleeves. How many shirts have long sleeves?<br><br>*Math Drawing:*<br><br>```
     84
    / \
   /   \
  39    □
```<br><br>*Situation Equation:*<br>$84 = 39 + \square$<br>*Solution Equation:*<br>$84 - 39 = \square$ | Of the 84 shirts in a clothing store, some have short sleeves. Forty-five have long sleeves. How many shirts have short sleeves?<br><br>*Math Drawing:*<br><br>```
     84
    / \
   /   \
  □     45
```<br><br>*Situation Equation:*<br>$84 = \square + 45$<br>*Solution Equation:*<br>$\square = 84 - 45$ |

| Both Addends Unknown is a productive extension of this basic situation, especially for small numbers less than or equal to 10. Such take apart situations can be used to show all the decompositions of a given number. The associated equations, which have a total on the left of the equal sign, help children understand that the = sign does not always mean *makes* or *results in* but always does mean *is the same number as.* | **Both Addends Unknown**

Pam has 24 roses. How many can she put in her red vase and how many in her blue vase?

Math Drawing:

Situation Equation:
$24 = \square + \square$ |

²These math drawings are called Math Mountains in Grades 1–3 and break-apart drawings in Grades 4 and 5.
```

Addition and Subtraction Problem Types (continued)

	Difference Unknown	Greater Unknown	Smaller Unknown
Compare[1]	Alex has 64 trading cards. Lucy has 48 trading cards. How many more trading cards does Alex have than Lucy? Lucy has 48 trading cards. Alex has 64 trading cards. How many fewer trading cards does Lucy have than Alex? *Math Drawing:* A ⟦ 64 ⟧ L ⟦ 48 ⟧ (?) *Situation Equation:* 48 + ☐ = 64 or ☐ = 64 − 48 *Solution Equation:* ☐ = 64 − 48	**Leading Language** Lucy has 48 trading cards. Alex has 16 more trading cards than Lucy. How many trading cards does Alex have? **Misleading Language** Lucy has 48 trading cards. Lucy has 16 fewer trading cards than Alex. How many trading cards does Alex have? *Math Drawing:* A ⟦ ? ⟧ L ⟦ 48 ⟧ (16) *Situation and Solution Equation:* 48 + 16 = ☐	**Leading Language** Alex has 64 trading cards. Lucy has 16 fewer trading cards than Alex. How many trading cards does Lucy have? **Misleading Language** Alex has 64 trading cards. Alex has 16 more trading cards than Lucy. How many trading cards does Lucy have? *Math Drawing:* A ⟦ 64 ⟧ L ⟦ ? ⟧ (16) *Situation Equation:* ☐ + 16 = 64 or ☐ = 64 − 16 *Solution Equation:* ☐ = 64 − 16

[1] A comparison sentence can always be said in two ways. One way uses *more*, and the other uses *fewer* or *less*. Misleading language suggests the wrong operation. For example, it says *Lucy has 16 fewer trading cards than Alex*, but you have to add 16 cards to the number of cards Lucy has to get the number of cards Alex has.

Glossary

5-groups*

|||| |||| tens in 5-groups

○○○○○
○○○○○ ones in 5-groups

A

add

•••• ••
4 + 2 = 6

addend

5 + 6 = 11
  ↑ ↑

addends

Adding Up Method* (for Subtraction)

$$\begin{array}{r} 144 \\ - 68 \\ \hline 76 \end{array}$$

$68 + 2 = 70$
$70 + 30 = 100$
$100 + 44 = 144$

$\boxed{76}$

addition doubles*

Both addends (or partners) are the same.

$4 + 4 = 8$

A.M.

Use A.M. for times between midnight and noon.

analog clock

angle

These are angles.

array

This rectangular array has 3 rows and 5 columns.

*A classroom research-based term developed for *Math Expressions*

B

bar graph

Coins in My Collection

| | | | | | | | | | | |
United States
Canada
Mexico
Japan
India
0 1 2 3 4 5 6 7 8 9 10

horizontal bar graph

Flowers in My Garden

10
9
8
7
6
5
4
3
2
1
0
Roses Daisies Violets Tulips Lilies

vertical bar graph

break-apart*

You can break apart a larger number to get two smaller amounts called break-aparts.

10
6   4

break-aparts of 10

C

cent

front   back

1 cent or 1¢ or $0.01

centimeter (cm)

1 cm

0   1   2   3   4

cent sign

56¢

↑

cent sign

clock

analog clock

digital clock   12:30

columns

This rectangular array has 4 columns with 3 tiles in each column.

*A classroom research-based term developed for *Math Expressions*

compare numbers

Compare numbers using >, <, or =.

52 > 25

25 < 52

25 = 25

comparison bars*

You can add labels and fill in numbers to help you solve *Compare* problems.

count all*

$$5 + 3 = \square$$

1 2 3 4 5 6 7 8

• • • • • • • •

$$5 + 3 = \boxed{8}$$

count on

$$5 + 3 = \boxed{8}$$

$$5 + \boxed{3} = 8$$

$$8 - 5 = \boxed{3}$$

Already 5

cube

data

	Sisters	Brothers
Kendra	2	1
Scott	2	0
Ida	0	1

data

The data in the table show how many sisters and how many brothers each child has.

decade numbers*

10, 20, 30, 40, 50, 60, 70, 80, 90

decimal point

$4.25

↑

decimal point

diagonal

diagonal

*A classroom research-based term developed for *Math Expressions*

difference

$$11 - 3 = 8$$

$$\begin{array}{r} 11 \\ -\ 3 \\ \hline 8 \end{array}$$

difference ⟶ 8

digital clock

12:30

digits

0, 1, 2, 3, 4, 5, 6, 7, 8, 9

15 is a 2-digit number.

The 1 in 15 means 1 ten.

The 5 in 15 means 5 ones.

dime

front   back

10 cents or 10¢ or $0.10

dollar

100 cents or
100¢ or $1.00

 front

 back

dollar sign

$4.25

↑

dollar sign

doubles minus 1

7 + 7 = 14, so

7 + 6 = 13, 1 less than 14.

doubles minus 2

7 + 7 = 14, so

7 + 5 = 12, 2 less than 14.

doubles plus 1

6 + 6 = 12, so

6 + 7 = 13, 1 more than 12.

doubles plus 2

6 + 6 = 12, so

6 + 8 = 14, 2 more than 12.

E

equal shares

2 halves   4 fourths

*A classroom research-based term developed for *Math Expressions*

equation

$$4 + 3 = 7 \qquad 7 = 4 + 3$$
$$9 - 5 = 4 \qquad 4 + 5 = 8 + 1$$

An equation must have an $=$ sign.

equation chain*

$$3 + 4 = 5 + 2 = 8 - 1 = 7$$

estimate

Make a reasonable guess about how many or how much.

even

A number is even if you can make groups of 2 and have none left over.

8 is an even number.

exact change

I will pay with 4 dimes and 3 pennies. That is the exact change. I won't get any money back.

expanded form

$$283 = 200 + 80 + 3$$

Expanded Method (for Addition)*

$$\begin{array}{r} 78 = 70 + 8 \\ + 57 = 50 + 7 \\ \hline 120 + 15 = 135 \end{array}$$

Expanded Method* (for Subtraction)

$$\begin{array}{r} 64 = \overset{50}{\cancel{60}} + \overset{14}{\cancel{4}} \\ - 28 = 20 + 8 \\ \hline 30 + 6 = 36 \end{array}$$

extra information

Franny has 8 kittens and 2 dogs. 4 kittens are asleep. How many kittens are awake?

$$8 - 4 = \boxed{4}$$

The number of dogs is extra information. It is not needed to solve the problem.

fewer

There are fewer ⬛ than △.

*A classroom research-based term developed for *Math Expressions*

foot (ft)

foot

12 inches = 1 foot   (not drawn to scale)

fourths

square

The picture shows 4 fourths. A fourth of the square is shaded.

G

greatest

25   41   63

63 is the greatest number.

group name*

flowers
─────
group name

H

half hour

5 minutes
10 minutes
15 minutes
20 minutes
25 minutes
30 minutes

30 minutes = 1 half hour

halves

square

The picture shows 2 halves. A half of the square is shaded.

hexagon

A hexagon has 6 sides and 6 angles.

*A classroom research-based term developed for *Math Expressions*

hidden information

Heather bought a dozen eggs. She used 7 of them to make breakfast. How many eggs does she have left?

$$12 - 7 = \boxed{5}$$

The hidden information is that a dozen means 12.

horizontal bar graph

Coins in My Collection

United States
Canada
Mexico
Japan
India

0 1 2 3 4 5 6 7 8 9 10

horizontal form

$$4 + 5 = 9$$

horizontal line

hour

60 minutes   5 minutes
55 minutes   10 minutes
50 minutes   15 minutes
45 minutes   20 minutes
40 minutes   25 minutes
35 minutes   30 minutes

60 minutes = 1 hour

hour hand

hour hand

hundreds

3 hundreds

347 has 3 hundreds.

↑

hundreds

I

inch (in.)

1 inch

0   1   2

is equal to (=)

$$5 + 3 = 8$$

5 plus 3 is equal to 8.

is greater than (>)

34   >   25

34 is greater than 25.

*A classroom research-based term developed for *Math Expressions*

is less than (<)

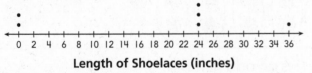

45   <   46

45 is less than 46.

L

least

14   7   63

7 is the least number.

length

The length of the pencil is about 17 cm.
(not to scale)

line plot

Length of Shoelaces (inches)

line segment

M

make a ten

$8 + 6 = \square$

8 •• | • • • •
10 + 4

10 + 4 = 14,

so 8 + 6 = 14

matching drawing*

fewer

more

Math Mountain*

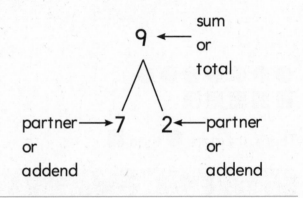

sum
or
total

partner ⟶ 7   2 ⟵ partner
or   or
addend   addend

meter (m)

100 centimeters = 1 meter
(not drawn to scale)

minus

$8 - 3 = 5$

$$\begin{array}{r} 8 \\ -3 \\ \hline 5 \end{array}$$

8 minus 3 equals 5.

minute

1 minute

60 seconds = 1 minute

*A classroom research-based term developed for *Math Expressions*

minute hand

minute hand: points to the minutes

more

There are more ⬤ than ⬛.

New Groups Above Method*

$$\overset{1}{56}$$
$$+ 28$$
$$\overline{84}$$

6 + 8 = 14
The 1 new ten in 14 goes up above the tens place.

New Groups Below Method*

$$56$$
$$+ 2\underset{1}{8}$$
$$\overline{84}$$

6 + 8 = 14
The 1 new ten in 14 goes below in the tens place.

nickel

front   back

5 cents or 5¢ or $0.05

not equal to (≠)

$$6 + 4 \neq 8$$

6 + 4 is not equal to 8.

number line diagram

This is a number line diagram.

number name

12

twelve ← number name

odd

A number is odd if you can make groups of 2 and have 1 left over.

9 is an odd number.

ones

7 ones

347 has 7 ones.

↑
ones

*A classroom research-based term developed for *Math Expressions*

opposite operations

Addition and subtraction are opposite operations.

$$5 + 9 = 14$$
$$14 - 9 = 5$$

Use addition to check subtraction. Use subtraction to check addition.

opposite sides

opposite sides

order

2, 5, 6

The numbers 2, 5, and 6 are in order from least to greatest.

P

pairs

A group of 2 is a pair.

The picture shows 4 pairs of counters.

partner lengths*

partner lengths of 4 cm

partners*

$$9 + 6 = 15$$

partners (addends)

pattern

This pattern shows counting by 2s.

2, 4, 6, 8, 10

penny

front   back

1 cent or 1¢ or $0.01

pentagon

A pentagon has 5 sides and 5 angles.

*A classroom research-based term developed for *Math Expressions*

picture graph

| Apples | 🍎🍎🍎🍎🍎🍎🍎 |
| Oranges | 🍊🍊🍊🍊🍊🍊🍊🍊🍊🍊 |

plus

$3 + 2 = 5$

3 plus 2 equals 5.

$$\begin{array}{r} 3 \\ +2 \\ \hline 5 \end{array}$$

P.M.

Use P.M. for times between noon and midnight.

proof drawing*

$86 + 57 = 143$

Q

quadrilateral

A quadrilateral has 4 sides and 4 angles.

quarter

front   back

25 cents or 25¢ or $0.25

A quarter is another name for a fourth.

A quarter is a fourth of a dollar.

quick hundreds*

347

quick hundreds

quick tens*

162

quick tens

R

rectangle

A rectangle has 4 sides and 4 right angles.
Opposite sides have the same length.

rectangular prism

*A classroom research-based term developed for *Math Expressions*

right angle

right angle

A right angle is sometimes called a *square corner*.

round

Express a number to the nearest ten or hundred. You can round down or round up.

$$52 \longrightarrow 50 \qquad 278 \longrightarrow 300$$

rows

This rectangular array has 3 rows with 4 tiles in each row.

ruler

A ruler is used to measure length.

S

scale

Coins in My Collection

scale

The numbers along the side or the bottom of a graph are the scale.

Show All Totals Method*

```
   25           724
 + 48         + 158
 ────         ─────
   60           800
   13            70
 ────            12
   73         ─────
                882
```

situation equation*

A baker baked 100 loaves of bread. He sold some loaves. There are 73 loaves left. How many loaves of bread did he sell?

$$100 - \boxed{} = 73$$

situation equation

*A classroom research-based term developed for *Math Expressions*

skip count

skip count by 2s: 2, 4, 6, 8, . . .
skip count by 5s: 5, 10, 15, 20, . . .
skip count by 10s: 10, 20, 30, 40, 50, . . .

solution equation*

A baker baked 100 loaves of bread. He sold some loaves. There are 73 loaves left. How many loaves of bread did he sell?

$$100 - 73 = \boxed{}$$

solution equation

square

A square has 4 equal sides and 4 right angles.

subtract

8 − 5 = 3

subtraction doubles*

The subtrahend and the difference, or partners, are the same.
8 − 4 = 4

sum

4 + 3 = 7

$$\begin{array}{r} 4 \\ + 3 \\ \hline 7 \end{array}$$

sum ⟶ 7

survey

When you collect data by asking people questions, you are taking a survey.

T

teen number

any number from 11 to 19

11 12 13 14 15 16 17 18 19

tens

4 tens

347 has 4 tens.

↑
tens

thirds

square

The picture shows 3 thirds. A third of the square is shaded.

*A classroom research-based term developed for *Math Expressions*

thousand

$1{,}000 = 10$ hundreds

total

10 ⟵ total

$8 \qquad 2$

triangle

A triangle has 3 sides and 3 angles.

U

ungroup*

Ungroup when you need more ones or tens to subtract.

Ungroup First Method*

$$\begin{array}{r} 6\,4 \\ -\,2\,8 \\ \hline \uparrow \ \ \uparrow \end{array}$$

yes no

1. Check to see if there are enough tens and ones to subtract.

$$\begin{array}{r} ^{5}\llap{}1^{14} \\ \cancel{6}\,\cancel{4} \\ -\,2\,8 \end{array}$$

2. You can get more ones by taking from the tens and putting them in the ones place.

$$\begin{array}{r} ^{5}\llap{}1^{14} \\ \cancel{6}\,\cancel{4} \\ -\,2\,8 \\ \hline 3\,6 \end{array}$$

3. Subtract from either right to left or left to right.

---

unknown addend

$3 +\ \boxed{}\ = 9$

↑

unknown addend

---

unknown total

$3 + 6 = \boxed{}$

↑

unknown total

V

vertical form

$$\begin{array}{r} 4 \\ +\,3 \\ \hline 7 \end{array}$$

*A classroom research-based term developed for *Math Expressions*

vertical bar graph

Flowers in My Garden

vertical line

view

This is the side view of the rectangular prism above.

width

width or length

length width

yard (yd)

3 feet = 1 yard

(not drawn to scale)

*A classroom research-based term developed for *Math Expressions*

2.OA Operations and Algebraic Thinking

Represent and solve problems involving addition and subtraction.

2.OA.A.1	Use addition and subtraction within 100 to solve one- and two-step word problems involving situations of adding to, taking from, putting together, taking apart, and comparing, with unknowns in all positions, e.g., by using drawings and equations with a symbol for the unknown number to represent the problem.	Unit 1 Lessons 1, 2, 4, 9, 10, 11, 12, 13, 14, 15, 16, 17, 18, 19, 20, 21; Unit 2 Lessons 1, 2, 6, 7, 8, 15; Unit 4 Lessons 3, 4, 5, 12, 13, 14, 16, 17, 18, 19, 20, 21, 22, 23; Unit 5 Lessons 3, 4, 5, 6, 7, 9, 10; Unit 6 Lesson 15; Unit 7 Lessons 3, 4, 5

Add and subtract within 20.

2.OA.B.2	Fluently add and subtract within 20 using mental strategies. By end of Grade 2, know from memory all sums of two one-digit numbers.	Unit 1 Lessons 1, 2, 3, 4, 5, 7, 8, 9, 10, 11, 12, 13, 14, 15, 16, 17, 18, 19, 20, 21; Unit 2 Lessons 2, 6; Unit 3 Lessons 1, 3, 4; Unit 4 Lessons 6, 13; Unit 5 Lessons 3, 4, 5, 6, 7, 8, 9, 10; Unit 7 Lesson 6

Work with equal groups of objects to gain foundations for multiplication.

2.OA.C.3	Determine whether a group of objects (up to 20) has an odd or even number of members, e.g., by pairing objects or counting them by 2s; write an equation to express an even number as a sum of two equal addends.	Unit 1 Lessons 6, 7, 21; Unit 7 Lesson 1
2.OA.C.4	Use addition to find the total number of objects arranged in rectangular arrays with up to 5 rows and up to 5 columns; write an equation to express the total as a sum of equal addends.	Unit 7 Lessons 1, 6

■ Major ■ Supporting ■ Additional

Common Core State Standards for Mathematical Content

2.NBT Number and Operations in Base Ten

Understand place value.

2.NBT.A.1	Understand that the three digits of a three-digit number represent amounts of hundreds, tens, and ones; e.g., 706 equals 7 hundreds, 0 tens, and 6 ones.	Unit 2 Lessons 1, 2, 3, 4, 5, 6, 7, 8, 9, 10, 11; Unit 4 Lessons 7, 8, 9, 10, 12; Unit 6 Lessons 1, 2, 3, 4, 10, 11, 12
2.NBT.A.1.a	Understand that the three digits of a three-digit number represent amounts of hundreds, tens, and ones; e.g., 706 equals 7 hundreds, 0 tens, and 6 ones. Understand the following as special cases: a. 100 can be thought of as a bundle of ten tens—called a "hundred."	Unit 2 Lessons 1, 2, 3, 4, 6, 7, 8, 9, 11; Unit 4 Lessons 3, 4, 7, 8, 9, 10, 12; Unit 6 Lessons 1, 4, 6, 7, 9. 10, 11, 13
2.NBT.A.1.b	Understand that the three digits of a three-digit number represent amounts of hundreds, tens, and ones; e.g., 706 equals 7 hundreds, 0 tens, and 6 ones. Understand the following as special cases: b. The numbers 100, 200, 300, 400, 500, 600, 700, 800, 900 refer to one, two, three, four, five, six, seven, eight, or nine hundreds (and 0 tens and 0 ones).	Unit 4 Lesson 7; Unit 6 Lesson 1
2.NBT.A.2	Count within 1000; skip-count by 5s, 10s, and 100s.	Unit 1 Lesson 6; Unit 2 Lessons 1, 2, 3, 12, 15; Unit 4 Lessons 1, 2, 15; Unit 5 Lesson 2; Unit 6 Lessons 1, 4
2.NBT.A.3	Read and write numbers to 1000 using base-ten numerals, number names, and expanded form.	Unit 2 Lessons 1, 2, 3, 4, 5; Unit 6 Lessons 1, 2, 4
2.NBT.A.4	Compare two three-digit numbers based on meanings of the hundreds, tens, and ones digits, using >, =, and < symbols to record the results of comparisons.	Unit 2 Lessons 5, 15; Unit 5 Lesson 10; Unit 6 Lessons 3, 15

■ Major   ■ Supporting   ■ Additional

2.NBT Number and Operations in Base Ten

Use place value understanding and properties of operations to add and subtract.

2.NBT.B.5	Fluently add and subtract within 100 using strategies based on place value, properties of operations, and/or the relationship between addition and subtraction.	Unit 2 Lessons 2, 4, 13, 14, 15; Unit 3 Lesson 9; Unit 4 Lessons 1, 2, 3, 4, 5, 6, 11, 12, 13, 14, 15, 16, 17, 18, 19, 20, 21, 22, 23; Unit 5 Lessons 5, 8, 9; Unit 6 Lessons 3, 8, 10, 15; Unit 7 Lessons 3, 4, 5
2.NBT.B.6	Add up to four two-digit numbers using strategies based on place value and properties of operations.	Unit 2 Lessons 6, 8, 9, 10, 14, 15; Unit 4 Lessons 3, 5, 12, 15, 16, 17, 18; Unit 7 Lessons 4, 5
2.NBT.B.7	Add and subtract within 1000, using concrete models or drawings and strategies based on place value, properties of operations, and/or the relationship between addition and subtraction; relate the strategy to a written method. Understand that in adding or subtracting three-digit numbers, one adds or subtracts hundreds and hundreds, tens and tens, ones and ones; and sometimes it is necessary to compose or decompose tens or hundreds.	Unit 2 Lessons 4, 6, 7, 8, 9, 10, 11, 14, 15; Unit 3 Lesson 6; Unit 4 Lessons 3, 4, 5, 6, 7, 8, 9, 10, 12, 13, 15, 16, 17, 18, 19, 20; Unit 6 Lessons 2, 4, 5, 6, 7, 8, 9, 10, 11, 12, 13, 14, 15
2.NBT.B.8	Mentally add 10 or 100 to a given number 100–900, and mentally subtract 10 or 100 from a given number 100–900.	Unit 2 Lesson 4; Unit 4 Lesson 15; Unit 6 Lessons 2, 4
2.NBT.B.9	Explain why addition and subtraction strategies work, using place value and the properties of operations.	Unit 1 Lessons 1, 3, 4, 5, 7, 9, 10, 11, 16, 20; Unit 2 Lessons 2, 4, 6, 7, 8, 9, 10; Unit 4 Lessons 3, 4, 5, 6, 7, 8, 9, 10, 12, 14, 15, 16, 17, 18; Unit 6 Lessons 2, 5, 6, 7, 8, 9, 10, 11, 12, 13, 14, 15; Unit 7 Lessons 4, 5

Common Core State Standards for Mathematical Content

2.MD Measurement and Data

Measure and estimate lengths in standard units.

2.MD.A.1	Measure the length of an object by selecting and using appropriate tools such as rulers, yardsticks, meter sticks, and measuring tapes.	Unit 3 Lessons 1, 2, 3, 4, 6, 7, 8, 9; Unit 4 Lesson 23; Unit 7 Lesson 1
2.MD.A.2	Measure the length of an object twice, using length units of different lengths for the two measurements; describe how the two measurements relate to the size of the unit chosen.	Unit 3 Lessons 7, 8, 9
2.MD.A.3	Estimate lengths using units of inches, feet, centimeters, and meters.	Unit 3 Lessons 3, 4, 6, 7, 8; Unit 4 Lesson 23
2.MD.A.4	Measure to determine how much longer one object is than another, expressing the length difference in terms of a standard length unit.	Unit 3 Lessons 1, 2, 6; Unit 4 Lesson 23

Relate addition and subtraction to length.

2.MD.B.5	Use addition and subtraction within 100 to solve word problems involving lengths that are given in the same units, e.g., by using drawings (such as drawings of rulers) and equations with a symbol for the unknown number to represent the problem.	Unit 4 Lesson 23; Unit 7 Lessons 3, 4, 5
2.MD.B.6	Represent whole numbers as lengths from 0 on a number line diagram with equally spaced points corresponding to the numbers 0, 1, 2, . . . , and represent whole-number sums and differences within 100 on a number line diagram.	Unit 7 Lessons 3, 5

Work with time and money.

2.MD.C.7	Tell and write time from analog and digital clocks to the nearest five minutes, using a.m. and p.m.	Unit 5 Lessons 1, 2
2.MD.C.8	Solve word problems involving dollar bills, quarters, dimes, nickels, and pennies, using $ and ¢ symbols appropriately. *Example: If you have 2 dimes and 3 pennies, how many cents do you have?*	Unit 2 Lessons 11, 12, 15; Unit 4 Lessons 1, 2, 10; Unit 5 Lessons 3, 4

■ **Major**   ■ **Supporting**   ■ **Additional**

2.MD Measurement and Data

Represent and interpret data.

2.MD.D.9	Generate measurement data by measuring lengths of several objects to the nearest whole unit, or by making repeated measurements of the same object. Show the measurements by making a line plot, where the horizontal scale is marked off in whole-number units.	Unit 3 Lessons 6, 7, 8
2.MD.D.10	Draw a picture graph and a bar graph (with single-unit scale) to represent a data set with up to four categories. Solve simple put-together, take-apart, and compare problems using information presented in a bar graph.	Unit 5 Lessons 3, 4, 5, 6, 7, 8, 9, 10

2.G Geometry

Reason with shapes and their attributes.

2.G.A.1	Recognize and draw shapes having specified attributes, such as a given number of angles or a given number of equal faces. Identify triangles, quadrilaterals, pentagons, hexagons, and cubes.	Unit 3 Lessons 2, 3, 4, 5, 9; Unit 7 Lessons 1, 2, 4, 5
2.G.A.2	Partition a rectangle into rows and columns of same-size squares and count to find the total number of them.	Unit 7 Lessons 1, 6
2.G.A.3	Partition circles and rectangles into two, three, or four equal shares, describe the shares using the words *halves*, *thirds*, *half of*, *a third of*, etc., and describe the whole as two halves, three thirds, four fourths. Recognize that equal shares of identical wholes need not have the same shape.	Unit 5 Lesson 2; Unit 7 Lessons 1, 2, 6

Common Core State Standards for Mathematical Practice

MP1 Make sense of problems and persevere in solving them.

Mathematically proficient students start by explaining to themselves the meaning of a problem and looking for entry points to its solution. They analyze givens, constraints, relationships, and goals. They make conjectures about the form and meaning of the solution and plan a solution pathway rather than simply jumping into a solution attempt. They consider analogous problems, and try special cases and simpler forms of the original problem in order to gain insight into its solution. They monitor and evaluate their progress and change course if necessary. Older students might, depending on the context of the problem, transform algebraic expressions or change the viewing window on their graphing calculator to get the information they need. Mathematically proficient students can explain correspondences between equations, verbal descriptions, tables, and graphs or draw diagrams of important features and relationships, graph data, and search for regularity or trends. Younger students might rely on using concrete objects or pictures to help conceptualize and solve a problem. Mathematically proficient students check their answers to problems using a different method, and they continually ask themselves, "Does this make sense?" They can understand the approaches of others to solving complex problems and identify correspondences between different approaches.

Unit 1 Lessons 2, 3, 4, 5, 6, 7, 9, 10, 11, 12, 13, 14, 15, 16, 17, 18, 19, 20, 21
Unit 2 Lessons 1, 3, 4, 5, 6, 7, 8, 9, 11, 12, 13, 14, 15
Unit 3 Lessons 1, 3, 6, 9
Unit 4 Lessons 1, 2, 3, 4, 5, 6, 7, 8, 9, 10, 11, 12, 13, 14, 16, 17, 18, 19, 20, 21, 22, 23
Unit 5 Lessons 1, 3, 4, 5, 6, 7, 8, 9, 10
Unit 6 Lessons 1, 4, 5, 8, 9, 10, 11, 12, 14, 15
Unit 7 Lessons 1, 2, 3, 4, 5, 6

MP2 Reason abstractly and quantitatively.

Mathematically proficient students make sense of quantities and their relationships in problem situations. They bring two complementary abilities to bear on problems involving quantitative relationships: the ability to *decontextualize*—to abstract a given situation and represent it symbolically and manipulate the representing symbols as if they have a life of their own, without necessarily attending to their referents— and the ability to *contextualize*, to pause as needed during the manipulation process in order to probe into the referents for the symbols involved. Quantitative reasoning entails habits of creating a coherent representation of the problem at hand, considering the units involved, attending to the meaning of quantities, not just how to compute them, and knowing and flexibly using different properties of operations and objects.

Unit 1 Lessons 1, 5, 7, 8, 9, 10, 11, 14, 21
Unit 2 Lessons 1, 3, 4, 5, 6, 7, 8, 9, 11, 12, 13, 14, 15
Unit 3 Lessons 1, 2, 3, 7, 8, 9
Unit 4 Lessons 1, 2, 3, 4, 5, 6, 7, 8, 9, 10, 11, 12, 13, 15, 17, 19, 20, 22, 23
Unit 5 Lessons 1, 2, 3, 5,10
Unit 6 Lessons 1, 2, 4, 10, 15
Unit 7 Lessons 1, 2, 3, 4, 5, 6

MP3 Construct viable arguments and critique the reasoning of others.

Mathematically proficient students understand and use stated assumptions, definitions, and previously established results in constructing arguments. They make conjectures and build a logical progression of statements to explore the truth of their conjectures. They are able to analyze situations by breaking them into cases, and can recognize and use counterexamples. They justify their conclusions, communicate them to others, and respond to the arguments of others. They reason inductively about data, making plausible arguments that take into account the context from which the data arose. Mathematically proficient students are also able to compare the effectiveness of two plausible arguments, distinguish correct logic or reasoning from that which is flawed, and—if there is a flaw in an argument—explain what it is. Elementary students can construct arguments using concrete referents such as objects, drawings, diagrams, and actions. Such arguments can make sense and be correct, even though they are not generalized or made formal until later grades. Later, students learn to determine domains to which an argument applies. Students at all grades can listen to or read the arguments of others, decide whether they make sense, and ask useful questions to clarify or improve the arguments.

Unit 1 Lessons 1, 2, 3, 4, 5, 6, 7, 8, 9, 10, 11, 12, 13, 14, 15, 16, 17, 18, 19, 20, 21
Unit 2 Lessons 1, 2, 3, 4, 5, 6, 7, 8, 9, 10, 11, 12, 13, 14, 15
Unit 3 Lessons 1, 2, 3, 4, 5, 6, 7, 8, 9
Unit 4 Lessons 1, 2, 3, 4, 5, 6, 7, 8, 9, 10, 11, 12, 13, 14, 15, 16, 17, 18, 19, 20, 21, 22, 23
Unit 5 Lessons 1, 2, 3, 4, 5, 6, 7, 8, 9, 10
Unit 6 Lessons 1, 2, 3, 4, 5, 6, 7, 8, 9, 10, 11, 12, 13, 14, 15
Unit 7 Lessons 1, 2, 3, 4, 5, 6

MP4 Model with mathematics.

Mathematically proficient students can apply the mathematics they know to solve problems arising in everyday life, society, and the workplace. In early grades, this might be as simple as writing an addition equation to describe a situation. In middle grades, a student might apply proportional reasoning to plan a school event or analyze a problem in the community. By high school, a student might use geometry to solve a design problem or use a function to describe how one quantity of interest depends on another. Mathematically proficient students who can apply what they know are comfortable making assumptions and approximations to simplify a complicated situation, realizing that these may need revision later. They are able to identify important quantities in a practical situation and map their relationships using such tools as diagrams, two-way tables, graphs, flowcharts and formulas. They can analyze those relationships mathematically to draw conclusions. They routinely interpret their mathematical results in the context of the situation and reflect on whether the results make sense, possibly improving the model if it has not served its purpose.

Unit 1 Lessons 10, 11, 12, 13, 14, 15, 16, 17, 18, 19, 20, 21
Unit 2 Lessons 1, 4, 6, 7, 11, 12, 14, 15
Unit 3 Lessons 6, 7, 8, 9
Unit 4 Lessons 1, 3, 4, 5, 7, 10, 12, 13, 18, 19, 20, 21, 23
Unit 5 Lessons 3, 5, 8, 9, 10
Unit 6 Lessons 9, 11, 14, 15
Unit 7 Lessons 3, 6

MP5 Use appropriate tools strategically.

Mathematically proficient students consider the available tools when solving a mathematical problem. These tools might include pencil and paper, concrete models, a ruler, a protractor, a calculator, a spreadsheet, a computer algebra system, a statistical package, or dynamic geometry software. Proficient students are sufficiently familiar with tools appropriate for their grade or course to make sound decisions about when each of these tools might be helpful, recognizing both the insight to be gained and their limitations. For example, mathematically proficient high school students analyze graphs of functions and solutions generated using a graphing calculator. They detect possible errors by strategically using estimation and other mathematical knowledge. When making mathematical models, they know that technology can enable them to visualize the results of varying assumptions, explore consequences, and compare predictions with data. Mathematically proficient students at various grade levels are able to identify relevant external mathematical resources, such as digital content located on a website, and use them to pose or solve problems. They are able to use technological tools to explore and deepen their understanding of concepts.

Unit 1 Lessons 3, 6, 20, 21
Unit 2 Lessons 1, 2, 3, 4, 5, 8, 12, 13, 14, 15
Unit 3 Lessons 1, 2, 3, 5, 6, 7, 8, 9
Unit 4 Lessons 1, 2, 3, 4, 7, 8, 9, 11, 18, 23
Unit 5 Lessons 1, 2, 5, 10
Unit 6 Lessons 1, 2, 5, 7, 10, 15
Unit 7 Lessons 1, 2, 3, 6

MP6 Attend to precision.

Mathematically proficient students try to communicate precisely to others. They try to use clear definitions in discussion with others and in their own reasoning. They state the meaning of the symbols they choose, including using the equal sign consistently and appropriately. They are careful about specifying units of measure and labeling axes to clarify the correspondence with quantities in a problem. They calculate accurately and efficiently, expressing numerical answers with a degree of precision appropriate for the problem context. In the elementary grades, students give carefully formulated explanations to each other. By the time they reach high school they have learned to examine claims and make explicit use of definitions.

Unit 1 Lessons 1, 2, 3, 4, 5, 6, 7, 8, 9, 10, 11, 12, 13, 14, 15, 16, 17, 18, 19, 20, 21
Unit 2 Lessons 1, 2, 3, 4, 5, 6, 7, 8, 9, 10, 11, 12, 13, 14, 15
Unit 3 Lessons 1, 2, 3, 4, 5, 6, 7, 8, 9
Unit 4 Lessons 1, 2, 3, 4, 5, 6, 7, 8, 9, 10, 11, 12, 13, 14, 15, 16, 17, 18, 19, 20, 21, 22, 23
Unit 5 Lessons 1, 2, 3, 4, 5, 6, 7, 8, 9, 10
Unit 6 Lessons 1, 2, 3, 4, 5, 6, 7, 8, 9, 10, 11, 12, 13, 14, 15
Unit 7 Lessons 1, 2, 3, 4, 5, 6

Common Core State Standards for Mathematical Practice

MP7 Look for and make use of structure.

Mathematically proficient students look closely to discern a pattern or structure. Young students, for example, might notice that three and seven more is the same amount as seven and three more, or they may sort a collection of shapes according to how many sides the shapes have. Later, students will see 7×8 equals the well remembered $7 \times 5 + 7 \times 3$, in preparation for learning about the distributive property. In the expression $x^2 + 9x + 14$, older students can see the 14 as 2×7 and the 9 as $2 + 7$. They recognize the significance of an existing line in a geometric figure and can use the strategy of drawing an auxiliary line for solving problems. They also can step back for an overview and shift perspective. They can see complicated things, such as some algebraic expressions, as single objects or as being composed of several objects. For example, they can see $5 - 3(x - y)^2$ as 5 minus a positive number times a square and use that to realize that its value cannot be more than 5 for any real numbers x and y.

Unit 1 Lessons 1, 2, 3, 5, 6, 9, 13, 17, 18, 19, 21
Unit 2 Lessons 1, 2, 3, 4, 6, 10, 11, 12, 15
Unit 3 Lessons 1, 3, 4, 5, 7, 8, 9
Unit 4 Lessons 1, 2, 7, 13, 17, 19, 21, 23
Unit 5 Lessons 2, 6, 7, 10
Unit 6 Lessons 4, 12, 13, 15
Unit 7 Lessons 2, 6

MP8 Look for and express regularity in repeated reasoning.

Mathematically proficient students notice if calculations are repeated, and look both for general methods and for shortcuts. Upper elementary students might notice when dividing 25 by 11 that they are repeating the same calculations over and over again, and conclude they have a repeating decimal. By paying attention to the calculation of slope as they repeatedly check whether points are on the line through (1, 2) with slope 3, middle school students might abstract the equation $(y - 2)/(x - 1) = 3$. Noticing the regularity in the way terms cancel when expanding $(x - 1)(x + 1)$, $(x - 1)(x^2 + x + 1)$, and $(x - 1)(x^3 + x^2 + x + 1)$ might lead them to the general formula for the sum of a geometric series. As they work to solve a problem, mathematically proficient students maintain oversight of the process, while attending to the details. They continually evaluate the reasonableness of their intermediate results.

Unit 1 Lessons 2, 6, 7, 21
Unit 2 Lessons 5, 10, 11, 15
Unit 3 Lessons 1, 2, 7, 8, 9
Unit 4 Lessons 4, 8, 13, 23
Unit 5 Lesson 10
Unit 6 Lessons 2, 4, 7, 8, 12, 15
Unit 7 Lessons 2, 6

Index

A

Addend, 3, 33–34, 333–334. *See also* **Partners; Unknown addends or partners.**

Adding Up Method, 235–238, 333–334

Addition
within 100, 292
within 1000, 349, 351–355
add 1, 91, 96
add 10s, 91, 95–96, 321
add 100, 96, 321
algorithms
  New Groups Below, 107–108, 328
  Show All Totals Method, 105
checking, 350
doubles, 26, 27–28
Fluency Check, 36, 58, 78, 100, 114, 132, 158, 182, 201, 226, 254, 274, 281, 300, 324, 336, 347, 357, 378, 394
fluency practice, 34, 48, 104, 123–124, 231, 238, 246, 284, 318, 342
grouping in, 103–104, 328, 329
model
  boxes, sticks, and circles, 328
  comparison bars, 69
  drawings, 39–45, 47–52, 63–70, 230, 243–245, 351–355
  equations, 50, 230, 243–245, 351–355
  Math Mountains, 5–6, 66, 67–68, 69–70, 227–228, 351–355
money amounts, 234
New Groups Below, 107–108, 328
number line diagram, 382, 390
properties
  Associative Property, 33
  Commutative Property, 4, 5–6, 29

relate to subtraction, 3–6, 227–228, 350
strategies
  count on, 4
  doubles, 26, 27–28
  doubles minus 1, 27–28
  doubles minus 2, 27–28
  doubles plus 1, 27–28
  doubles plus 2, 27–28
  make a ten, 17–18, 53–56
  proof drawings, 105–106, 107–108, 110–112, 124, 128, 330
three or more addends
  single-digit addends, 33–34, 149–152
  two-digit addends, 127–128, 384–387
totals to 1,000, 321–322, 327–330
totals to 20, 3–6, 13–14, 17, 19–21, 26, 27–28, 30, 88
totals to 200, 103–104, 105–106, 107–108, 109–110, 111–112, 227–228
unknown addends, 19–21. *See also* Problem Types.
vertical form, 30
word problems. *See* Problem Solving; Problem Types; Word Problems.

Algebra. *See also* **Addition; Equations; Problem Types; Subtraction.**
equations and inequalities
  modeling equations, 3, 5–6, 50, 51–52, 63–64, 230
  writing an equation, 30, 50, 51–52, 63–64, 67–68, 241–242, 243–255, 369
  writing a related equation, 5–6
meaning of equality, 30, 47

properties
  Associative, 33–34
  Commutative (addition), 4, 5–6, 29
symbols showing relations. *See* Symbols.
unknown addends, 13–14, 19–20, 21–22, 47, 237–238, 239–240, 241–242, 243–244, 333–334, 390. *See also* Problem Solving.

Algorithms
addition
  New Groups Below, 107–108, 109–110, 328
  regrouping, 109–110
  Show All Totals Method, 105–106
subtraction
  Expanded Method, 209, 211, 213, 339–340
  ungroup, 203–204, 215–216
  Ungroup First Method, 210, 339–340, 341, 344, 345–346, 349

Angles, 145–146

Arrays, 369

Assessment
Fluency Check, 36, 58, 78, 100, 114, 132, 158, 182, 202, 226, 254, 274, 281, 300, 324, 336, 348, 358, 378, 394
Formative Assessment
  Performance Task, 83–84, 137–138, 187–188, 259–260, 305–306, 363–364, 399–400
  Unit Review/Test, 79–82, 133–136, 183–186, 255–258, 301–304, 359–362, 395–398
Quick Quiz, 35, 57, 77, 99, 113, 131, 157, 181, 201, 225, 253, 273, 281, 299, 323, 335, 347, 357, 377, 393

B

Bar Graphs. *See also* **Word Problems.**
horizontal, 283, 285–286, 288
making, 283, 286, 289, 291, 293, 297–298
reading, 285–286, 293
solve word problems using, 287–288, 294–295
vertical, 285–286, 289

Base ten blocks
representing numbers, 93, 311–312

C

Centimeter, 141–144, 149–150, 151–152, 163–164, 174–178

Cent sign (¢), 117, 219–220

Clock. *See also* **Time**

Coins
count, 117, 199–200
dime, 117, 122
nickel, 120–122
penny, 117, 121–122
quarter, 193–194
value of coins and bills, 117, 120–122

Common Core Standards
Mathematical Content correlation, S19–S27. *See also* beginning of each lesson.

Commutative Property (addition), 4, 5–6, 29

Compare
graphs, 291
measurement units, 163, 173–174, 174–178
numbers, 97–98, 317–318

Index

plane shapes, 145–148

using graphs, 279, 286

Compare Word Problems. *See* **Problem Types.**

Comparison. *See also* **Problem Types; Symbols.**

language. *See also* Symbols.

fewer, 47–48, 49, 63, 241, 279, 295–296

more, 47–48, 49, 63, 241, 279, 295–296

word problems, 241–242

Comparison bars, 47–48, 49–50, 63–64, 65, 69, 241–242, 296

Counting

by 2s, 23–24

by 5s, 119–122, 269

by 10s, 87, 93, 122, 319

by 100s, 309, 315

money, 117–122, 120–122

over the hundreds, 319

Count On Strategy. *See* **Addition: strategies; Subtraction: strategies.**

Cubes, 155–156

Customary Units of Measurement. *See* **Measurement.**

D

Data. *See also* **Bar graphs; Picture Graphs; Word Problems.**

collect, 164, 170, 173, 178, 283, 291, 298

organize, 291

represent, 164–166, 177, 293, 296

tables, 149–150, 151–152, 164, 170, 291, 293

Decimal notation, 220

Dime, 117, 122

Dollar, 115–116

place value representation, 220

value of, 117–118

Dollar equivalents, 197–198

Dollar sign ($), 117, 220

Dollars with Penny Array, 309–310

Dot plots, 165–166, 174–177

Drawing

for addition, 39–40, 41–42, 43–44, 45, 47–52, 328, 330, 351–355

comparison bars, 47–50, 63–65, 69, 241–242, 246, 296

Math Mountains, 6, 30

money amounts, 122, 195–196

numbers, 94, 97–98, 315

proof drawings, 105–106, 107–108, 109–110, 111–112, 124, 128, 212, 230, 322, 328, 330, 339

rectangular prisms, 155

for subtraction, 203–204, 339, 344–346, 349, 351–355

E

Equal shares

fourths, 371–372, 375–376, 391–392

halves, 371–372, 375–376

thirds, 371–372, 375–376

Equal sign (=), 29, 97–98, 317

Equations. *See also* **Addition; Algebra; Problem Types; Subtraction.**

chains, 29

relate to Math Mountains, 3, 66–67, 227–228, 229–230. *See also* Subtraction.

situation and solution, S1–S3

unknown addend or partner, 30,
230, 237–240, 333–334. *See also*
Subtraction.
unknown total, 13–14, 30, 47–48,
67, 96, 227–228, 241–242,
243–245, 390
vertical form, 30

Estimation
length, 149–150, 151–152, 163–164,
170, 173

Even numbers, 25–26

Expanded form, 93, 316

Expanded Method
in subtraction. *See* Algorithms.

F

**Family Letter, 1–2, 7–8, 37–38, 85–86,
101–102, 139–140, 159–160, 189–
190, 261–262, 275–276, 307–308,
325–326, 337–338, 365–366**

Fluency activities and games
New Ten Challenge, 125–126
Ungroup Challenge, 223–224

Fluency
addition within 20, 34, 48, 104
addition within 100, 123–124,
231, 238, 246, 284, 318, 334,
342
Check, 36, 58, 78, 100, 114, 132,
158, 182, 202, 226, 254, 274, 281,
300, 324, 336, 348, 358, 378, 394
Path to Fluency, 36, 58, 100, 114,
132, 158, 182, 201, 226, 254, 274,
281, 300, 324, 336, 347, 357, 378,
394
subtraction within 20, 34, 48, 104
subtraction within 100, 221–222,
231, 238, 246, 334, 342

**Focus on Mathematical Practices,
75–76, 129–130, 179–180, 251–252
297–298, 355–356, 391–392**

Fourths, 371–372, 375–376

Fractions
equal shares, 371–372, 375–376,
391–392

G

Geometry. *See also* Measurement.
angles, 145–148, 156
right, 145–146, 149–150
attributes
corners (angles), 145–148
faces, 155–156
sides, 145–148, 156
plane shapes
circle, 376
classify, 145–148, 156
compare, 146–148
compose, 179–180
decompose, 179–180, 370–372,
375–376, 391–392
distance around (perimeter),
149–150, 151–152
hexagon, 148, 156, 179–180
measurement of, 149–150,
151–152
pentagon, 148, 156, 179–180
quadrilaterals, 148, 156, 179–180
rectangle, 146, 150, 155–156,
369–372, 375–376
square, 145–146, 149, 155–156,
376
triangle, 147, 151–152, 156,
179–180
solid shapes
build/combine, 155
classify, 156
cube, 155

nets, 153
rectangular prism, 153–156
relating to 2-D shapes, 156
sort, 156

Graphs. *See* **Bar graphs; Picture graphs; Word Problems.**

Grouping
in addition, 330

H

Halves, 371–372, 375–376

I

Inequality, 97–98, 317–318

L

Line plot, 165–166, 177

Line segment
draw, 142
measure with a ruler, 141–142

M

Manipulatives and materials
Blue Make-a-Ten Cards, 71–74
Circles and Rectangles, 373–374
Clock, 265–266
Coin Cards, 191–192
Coin Strips, 15–16
Dive the Deep, 31–32
Dollar Bills, 115–116
Dollar Equivalents, 197–198
Dollars with Penny Array, 309–310
Farm Stand, 118
Games
Find the Hidden Animal, 331–332
New Ten Challenge, 125–126
Ungroup Challenge, 223–224

Green Make-a-Ten Cards, 53–56
Juice Bar, 233–234
Math Mountain Cards, 9–12
Measuring tools
Inch Ruler, 167–168
Inch Tiles, 367–368
Meter Tape, 161–162
Yardstick, 171–172
Number Chart, 94, 320
Quarter Squares, 193–194
Rectangular Prisms (including cubes), 155–156
Secret Code Cards, 322
1 to 100, 89–90
200 to 1000, 313–314
Square-Inch Tiles, 367–368

Mathematical statements
use methods of proof, 81, 127, 178, 251–252, 297

Math Mountains
make-a-ten, 18
relate to equations, 3–6, 47–48, 49–50, 51–52, 66–68, 69–70, 227–228, 229–230
unknown addend or partner, 19–21, 351
unknown total, 350, 351

Measurement. *See also* **Estimation; Geometry; Time.**
height, 164
directly compare, 174, 175–177
length
compare, 141–143, 149, 174, 175–178, 251–252
directly compare, 178
iterate, 142–143
length units, 174, 175–178, 379–389
customary units, 169–170, 173–177

metric units, 141–144, 163, 170, 174, 175–176
  select a unit, 173
tools
  centimeter ruler, 141–143
  inch ruler, 169–170
  meter stick, 163
  yardstick, 171, 173
word problems, 379–383, 387–389
perimeter
  estimate, 149–152
  word problems, 384–386
tell and write time
  five minutes, 271–272
  half hour, 270
  hour, 267–268
time
  analog clocks, 263–264
  digital clocks, 263–264

Mental math, 95–96, 123–124, 223–224, 321

Meter, 163

Metric System. *See* Measurement.

Money, 233–234
change from one dollar, 234
coins. *See also* Manipulatives and materials.
  count, 120–122, 199–200, 219
  dime, 117, 122, 195–196
  nickel, 120–122, 195–196
  penny, 117, 121–122, 195–196
  quarter, 193–194, 195–196
  value of, 120–122, 199–200
count the value of coins and bills, 117–118, 120–122, 199–200
decimal notation, 220
dollars
  place value, 200
  value of, 117–118

place value, 200
symbols
  cent sign, 117, 219–220
  decimal notation, 220
  dollar sign, 117, 220
word problems, 117, 233–234, 249

Multiplication readiness, skip-counting
by 2s, 23–24
by 5s, 119–122, 269
by 10s, 87, 93, 122, 319
by 100s, 309, 315
arrays, 369–370

New Groups Below Method, 107–108, 109, 328

Nickel, 120–122

Number-Bond diagram. *See* Math Mountains.

Number line diagram
addition, 382, 390
subtraction, 382, 390

Number names, 94, 320

Number Path, 94

Numbers. *See also* Counting.
1 through 90, 94
11 through 20, 26, 27–28
101 to 1,000, 87, 93–94, 311–312, 315–316, 317–318, 319–320, 321–322
compare, 97–98, 317–318
decade numbers, 95
doubles, 26–28
even, 25–26
expanded form, 93, 316
fractions (even shares)
  fourths, 371–372, 375–376

halves, 270, 371–372
thirds, 371–372, 375
odd, 25–26
represent, 311–312, 315
word names for, 94, 320
writing, 87, 94, 320

O

Odd numbers, 23–26

Opposite operation, 350–351

P

Partners. *See also* **Addend.**
decade partners of, 95, 344, 345–346, 349
unknown partner, 13–14, 19–21, 30, 239–240, 241, 333–334

Patterns. *See* **Skip Counting.**
in equations, 4

Penny, 117, 121–122

Performance Task, 83–84, 137–138, 187–188, 259–260, 305–306, 363–364, 399–400

Perimeter, 149–150, 151–152, 384–386

Picture graphs
making, 277–278, 283, 291, 293
reading, 279–280, 297
solve word problems using, 297

Place value
drawings
circle, 97–98
quick hundreds, 97–98, 107, 109, 315, 317
quick tens, 92, 97–98
money, 220

Predict, 107–108, 110

Problem Solving. *See also* **Problem Types.**
distance around, 149–150, 151–152, 384–386
extra information, 60, 62, 70, 76
group name, 47–48, 95
hidden information, 62
measurement, 379–382, 383–386, 387–389
money, 200, 219, 234
not enough information, 59, 62
ones, tens, and hundreds, 321–322
real world problems, 75–76
subtraction (ungroup), 203–204
too much information, 60, 62, 70, 76
two-step, 65–66, 67–68, 106, 247–250, 288
unknown addends, 13–14, 19–21, 30, 39–40, 46, 47–48, 51–52, 203, 237–238, 239–240, 333–334
unknown total, 42, 44, 47–48, 70
use a graph, 287–288, 294–295, 297
write an equation, 67–68, 228, 229–230, 243–245
write a word problem, 59, 76, 291

Problem Types, S1–S3
Add To with Change Unknown, 3, 39–40, 41–42, 51–52
Add To with Result Unknown, 3, 39–40, 41–42, 70, 92, 107–108, 109–110, 111–112, 232–233
Add To with Start Unknown, 46, 70, 243–244
Compare with Bigger Unknown, 47–48, 49–50, 63–64, 69, 241, 245
Compare with Difference Unknown, 47–48, 49–50, 51–52, 63–64, 241–242, 244–245, 283, 296

Compare with Smaller Unknown, 47–48, 49–50, 51–52, 63–64, 241–242, 243–245

Compare with Total Unknown, 296

Put Together/Take Apart with Addend Unknown, 47–48, 51–52, 70, 237–238, 243

Put Together/Take Apart with Both Addends Unknown, 47, 51–52, 144, 244

Put Together/Take Apart with Total Unknown, 47–48, 103–106, 150, 151–152, 227–228, 243, 280, 283, 383, 384–386

Take From with Change Unknown, 42, 46, 245

Take From with Result Unknown, 3, 42, 46

Take From with Start Unknown, 46, 50, 69, 243–244

Two-step Problems, 65–66, 67–68, 106, 247–248, 249–250, 288

Proof Drawings. *See* **Drawing.**

Properties
Associative, 33
Commutative, 4, 230

Put Together/Take Apart Word Problems. *See* **Problem Types.**

Puzzled Penguin, 24, 29, 50, 70, 98, 110–112, 164, 200, 246, 272, 289, 292, 317, 344, 390

Q

Quadrilaterals, 145–146, 150, 376.
See also **Geometry.**

Quarter, 193–194

Quick Quiz, 35, 57, 77, 99, 113, 131, 157, 181, 201, 225, 253, 273, 281, 299, 323, 335, 347, 357, 377, 393

R

Rectangle, 146, 150, 369, 375

Rectangular arrays, 369

Rectangular prisms, 153–154, 155–156

Regroup, 109

Representing numbers
base ten blocks, 93, 315
boxes, sticks, circles, 315, 317
words, 94, 320

Right angle, 145–146

Ruler
centimeter ruler, 141–143, 163
inch ruler, 169–170
meter stick, 163–164, 251
yardstick, 171–174

S

Secret Code Cards, 322
1 to 100, 89–90
200 to 1000, 313–314

Shapes. *See* **Geometry.**

Show All Totals Method, 105

Skip counting
by 2s, 23–24
by 5s, 119–122, 269
by 10s, 87, 93, 122, 319
by 100s, 309, 315

Sort, 156, 291

Spatial reasoning, 155, 156

Square, 145, 149, 156, 179, 376

Square-Inch Tiles, 367–368

Standard units of measurement.
See **Measurement.**

Subtraction
3-digit numbers, 342–343, 344
within 20, 34, 92, 223–224, 230, 243, 321–322
within 100, 203–204, 221–222, 231, 284, 292, 334
within 1000, 344–345, 346, 349, 351–354, 355–356
accessible algorithms
Expanded Method, 206, 211, 337–338, 339–340
Ungroup First Method, 227–228, 337–338, 339–340, 341, 344, 345–346, 349
across zeros, 342
checking, 5, 220, 221–222, 350
difference, 341
Fluency Check, 36, 58, 78, 100, 114, 132, 158, 182, 201, 254, 274, 281, 300, 324, 336, 347, 357, 378, 394
fluency games and activities, 223–224, 331–332
fluency practice. *See* Fluency practice.
from hundreds numbers, 203–204
model
drawings, 230, 351–355
equations. *See* Algebra, 351–355
Math Mountains, 5–6, 66–70, 227–228, 351–354, 355
money amounts, 219–220
number line diagram, 382, 390
relate to addition, 3–6, 13–14, 230, 350
Secret Code Cards, 89–90, 313–314
situation and solution equations, 50
strategies
Adding Up Method, 235–236, 237– 238, 333–334
count on, 4
make a ten, 18, 71–74

proof drawings, 230, 339, 344, 345–346, 349
totals to 20, 3–6, 13–14, 88
totals to 100, 232, 233
understand subtraction as an unknown addend problem, 241–244, 333–334
ungrouping in, 203–204, 227–228, 344, 345–346, 349
unknown addend or partner. *See* Algebra; Equations; Problem Solving.
vertical form. *See* Equations.
within 1000, 339–340
word problems. *See also* Problem Solving; Problem Types; Word Problems.
solve with drawings, 39–40, 41–42, 43–44, 45, 47–48, 49–50, 51–52, 63–64, 67–68, 69, 203
solve with equations, 39–40, 41–42, 43–44, 45, 47–48, 49–50, 51–52, 63–64, 67–68, 69, 227–228
zero in the ones or tens place, 342

Symbols
cent sign (¢), 117, 219–220
dollar sign ($), 117, 220
equal sign (=), 29, 97–98, 317–318
is greater than (>), 97–98, 317–318
is less than (<), 97–98, 317–318
right angle, 145
unknown (?), 30

T

Take From Word Problems. *See* **Problem Types.**

Tape diagrams. *See* **Comparison bars.**

Three-dimensional figures. *See* **Geometry: solid shapes.**

Time
A.M./P.M., 264, 272
analog/digital clock, 263–264, 267–268
to five minutes, 271–272
half hour, 270
to the hour, 267–268
hour hand, 263, 267–268
minute hand, 263, 267–268, 270–272
minutes in an hour, 269, 271–272
unit relationships, 272

Triangle, 147, 151–152, 156

Two-dimensional figure. *See*
Geometry: plain shapes.

Two-step problems, 65–68, 106, 247–250, 288

U

Ungroup, 203–204

Ungroup Challenge, 223–224

Ungroup First Method, 339–340, 341, 344, 345–346, 349

Unit Review/Test, 79–82, 133–136, 183–186, 255–258, 301–304, 359–362, 395–398

Unknown addends or partners, 13–14, 19–20, 21, 47, 51–52, 66, 68, 69–70
addition, 237–238, 239–240, 241–242, 243
count on, 203
subtraction, 203, 243, 390
word problems, 237–238, 239–240, 333–334

V

Vertical form. *See* **Equations.**

Visual thinking, 155, 156

Vocabulary Cards, 2A–2F, 86A–86F, 140A–140F, 190A–190F, 262A–262F, 308A–308F, 366A–366F

W

What's the Error? 24, 29, 70, 98, 110–112, 164, 200, 246, 272, 289, 292, 317, 344, 390

Word problems, 3, 5, 39–45, 59–70, 75–76, 103–106, 203, 205–206, 218, 227–228, 235–236, 238, 243–245, 322, 327, 333–334, 339, 340, 351. *See also* **Problem Solving; Problem Types.**
compare methods, 129–130
compare word problems, 241–242
complex problems, 239–240
with groups of 10, 95
mixed, 49–50, 51–52, 67–68, 88, 92, 352–354, 355–356
two-step problems, 247–248, 249– 250
using data from a graph, 279–280, 287–288, 291, 294–295, 297–298
using length, 379–382, 383–386, 387–389

Z

Zero, 342
subtraction with, 342

Be an Illustrator

Illustrator: Josh Brill

Did you ever try to use shapes to draw animals like the platypus on the cover?

Over the last 10 years Josh has been using geometric shapes to design his animals. His aim is to keep the animal drawings simple and use color to make them appealing.

Add some color to the platypus Josh drew. Then try drawing a cat or dog or some other animal using the shapes below.

Shape Toolbox